M000266309

30+ Block Designs ◆ 14 Projects ◆ Easy Piecing Technique

mini-mosaic
QUILTS

PAULA DOYLE

C&T PUBLISHING

Text copyright © 2012 by Paula Doyle

Photography and Artwork copyright © 2012 by C&T Publishing, Inc.

Publisher: Amy Marson

Creative Director: Gailen Runge

Art Director: Kristy Zacharias

Editors: Lynn Koolish and Jill Mordick

Technical Editors: Sandy Peterson and Janice Wray

Cover/Book Designer: April Mostek

Production Coordinator: Jessica Jenkins

Production Editor: Alice Mace Nakanishi

Illustrator: Wendy Mathson

Photography by Christina Carty-Francis and Diane Pedersen of C&T Publishing, Inc., unless otherwise noted

Published by C&T Publishing, Inc., P.O. Box 1456, Lafayette, CA 94549

All rights reserved. No part of this work covered by the copyright hereon may be used in any form or reproduced by any means—graphic, electronic, or mechanical, including photocopying, recording, taping, or information storage and retrieval systems—without written permission from the publisher. The copyrights on individual artworks are retained by the artists as noted in *Mini-Mosaic Quilts*. These designs may be used to make items only for personal use or donation to nonprofit groups for sale or for display only at events, provided the following credit is included on a conspicuous label: Designs copyright © 2012 by Paula Doyle from the book *Mini-Mosaic Quilts* from C&T Publishing, Inc. Permission for all other purposes must be requested in writing from C&T Publishing, Inc.

Attention Copy Shops: Please note the following exception—publisher and author give permission to photocopy pages 11, 51, 66, 68, and 72, and pattern pullout pages P1 and P2 for personal use only.

Attention Teachers: C&T Publishing, Inc., encourages you to use this book as a text for teaching. Contact us at 800-284-1114 or www.ctpub.com for lesson plans and information about the C&T Creative Troupe.

We take great care to ensure that the information included in our products is accurate and presented in good faith, but no warranty is provided nor are results guaranteed. Having no control over the choices of materials or procedures used, neither the author nor C&T Publishing, Inc., shall have any liability to any person or entity with respect to any loss or damage caused directly or indirectly by the information contained in this book. For your convenience, we post an up-to-date listing of corrections on our website (www.ctpub.com). If a correction is not already noted, please contact our customer service department at ctinfo@ctpub.com or at P.O. Box 1456, Lafayette, CA 94549.

Trademark (™) and registered trademark (®) names are used throughout this book. Rather than use the symbols with every occurrence of a trademark or registered trademark name, we are using the names only in the editorial fashion and to the benefit of the owner, with no intention of infringement.

Library of Congress Cataloging-in-Publication Data

Doyle, Paula, 1954-

  Mini-mosaic quilts : 30+ block designs - 14 projects - easy piecing technique / Paula Doyle.

       pages cm

  ISBN 978-1-60705-361-3 (soft cover)

1. Patchwork--Patterns. 2. Quilting--Patterns. 3. Machine quilting. I. Title.

  TT835.D715 2012

  746.46--dc23

                    2012007865

Printed in China

10 9 8 7 6 5 4 3 2 1

dedication

This book is dedicated to the following people:

My amazing mother, Beverly Ann Warner Walter, who patiently taught me how to use a sewing machine when I was an impatient adolescent

My wonderful husband, Mark Doyle, and my son, Jonathan Doyle, who encourage me every day to do my best, and whose unfailing love and support have made it possible for me to be a full-time quilter

My grandmothers, Gertrude May Nims Warner and Stella Walter, both quilters, and all the talented quilters past and present who inspire me every day with their generosity of spirit and their stunning creations

acknowledgments

To Isabel Hall Kennedy and Mandy Parks, my two right-hand gals, thank you for your help in sewing all the blocks for the Tesserae Sampler Quilt for this book, for your ongoing feedback throughout, and for tirelessly demonstrating the Mini-Mosaic technique to hundreds of quilters. Thank you also to Monica Hauting for helping with the Darting Birds Neck Roll Cushion and to Kathleen Bull for helping to make the Tess the Starlet Sewing Box and the Zigzag Wallet. And finally, thank you to Pam Thompson and Venetta Morger for your enthusiastic support and encouragement in developing the concept of Mini-Mosaics, as well as helping with sewing the Rosebud Row and Friendship Star Chain patterns.

In addition to the friends who helped with all the stitching, I want to acknowledge Oakshott fabrics for supplying the wonderful hand-made Lipari line of shot fabrics used in making the Lipari Pinwheel Laptop Bag.

contents

INTRODUCTION

I've always loved small, intricate-looking quilt blocks. When I discovered foundation paper piecing in 1992 it was a "Eureka!" moment for me and opened a whole world of small-scale possibilities. Next time a space became available I signed up for a workshop on foundation piecing at my local quilt shop and found out about all the different block patterns I could make with this wonderful technique. But during that workshop I also found out about all the types of blocks that could not be easily made with the technique, including several of my favorites, such as Ohio Star and Card Trick.

Several years later I watched an episode of *Simply Quilts* with Alex Anderson in which one of the guest teachers stuck squares of fabric in a grid pattern onto fusible interfacing and then simply folded the interfacing and stitched the seams to connect the patchwork squares perfectly. A few months after that I remembered this technique when I was working on a project to which I wanted to add a little 3½˝ Trip Around the World block. I quickly rotary cut some 1˝ squares of fabric and then positioned and ironed them onto some fusible interfacing. I folded the interfacing along the lines where the raw edges of the fabric squares met and stitched ¼˝ away from the folded edge of the interfacing. The little block of ½˝ squares was done perfectly in no time at all! I was so excited that before I knew what was happening I'd produced a little doll's quilt in the same pattern.

Then I thought if I could just substitute simple pieced squares for some of the plain squares, I would have even more pattern possibilities with this technique, making possible many of those previously unobtainable small-scale block patterns! From then on, many of my waking hours were spent dreaming up quick and easy ways of making those pieced square tiles. I started with simple rotary-cut strips of fabric stitched together into sets, and then I used rotary-cut squares of freezer paper positioned and ironed in place onto the fabric sets as a template. To cut out a perfectly pieced tile, all I needed to do was to cut around the edge of the freezer paper template square with my scissors and lift it off. The result was perfect tiles, with no dog-ears to trim off and no annoying fabric fraying. Also, I found that although I wanted to use a lot of different yummy fabrics in my creations, I didn't need huge amounts, so fat quarters were especially handy to use—so much so that often the patterns in this book call for fat quarters in the yardage requirements. I find it so satisfying going into quilt shops and coming out with treasure troves of fat quarters for my projects without breaking the bank!

And so the concept of Mini-Mosaics patchwork for quilted projects was born. I hope you enjoy using this book as much as I have enjoyed writing it.

making the mini-mosaic
FABRIC TILES

selecting fabric for mini-mosaics

Fat quarters and fat eighths of fabrics are great for use in Mini-Mosaic projects—so much so that typically the patterns in this book instruct you to rotary cut strips that are half the full width of fabric (usually from 40″ to 45″). Use good-quality 100% cotton fabrics. Stick to plain, tone-on-tone, or hand-dyed fabrics; single-color batiks; or very small prints. Also keep the contrast level between the fabrics very high. The fabric pieces in Mini-Mosaics end up being very small in the finished article, so similar values of fabric will not stand out well if they are placed next to each other.

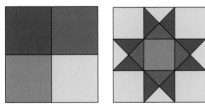

Low-contrast fabric selection

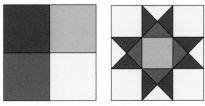

High-contrast fabric selection

cutting fabric strips

Rotary cut all of the strips of fabric used in the Mini-Mosaic tiles across the width of the fabric on the crosswise grain.

A fat quarter (18″ × 21″) yields about 17–18 strips 1″ × 21″ or 11–12 strips 1½″ × 21″. Since fat quarter sizes can vary, in this book a fat quarter is assumed to be 17″ × 20″.

A fat eighth (9″ × 21″) yields about 8–9 strips 1″ × 21″ or 5–6 strips 1½″ × 21″. Since fat eighth sizes can vary, in this book a fat eighth is assumed to be 8½″ × 20″.

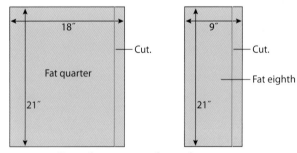

Cut strips on crosswise grain.

TIP

The June Tailor Shape Cut ruler is a useful tool for rotary cutting multiple strips or squares.

cutting freezer-paper tile templates

A freezer-paper template is needed to make each of the pieced Mini-Mosaic tiles, with the exception of the half-square rectangle tiles (below and page 7). Rotary cut the freezer paper into strips (1″ wide for Little Tile templates and 1½″ wide for Big Tile templates), and then rotary cut the strips into squares measuring 1″ × 1″ for Little Tile templates or 1½″ × 1½″ for Big Tile templates. Again, the June Tailor Shape Cut ruler is useful for cutting multiple strips and squares. The freezer-paper templates can each be used several times.

making mini-mosaic little tiles

All the Mini-Mosaic Little Tiles start out measuring 1″ × 1″ square from raw edge to raw edge, and finish up measuring ½″ × ½″ square after stitching. Only the simpler types of pieced tiles are suitable for this size of Mini-Mosaic, so patterns are limited to plain tiles, half-square rectangle tiles, half-square triangle tiles, and satin-stitched stem tiles.

Making Plain Little Tiles

Rotary cut strips of fabric 1″ × 20″ and then cut into 1″ × 1″ square tiles. Each strip yields 19–20 plain Little Tiles.

Making Pieced Little Tiles

MAKING HALF-SQUARE RECTANGLE LITTLE TILES

1. Rotary cut 2 strips of fabric ¾″ × 20″.

2. Stitch the 2 strips, right sides together, lengthwise, using a ¼″ seam allowance. Press the seam allowances open.

3. Rotary cut the strip set into 1″ × 1″ square tiles.

Each strip set will yield approximately 19–20 half-square rectangle Little Tiles.

MAKING HALF-SQUARE TRIANGLE LITTLE TILES

1. Rotary cut 2 fabric strips 1″ × 20″.

2. Stitch the 2 strips, right sides together, lengthwise, using a ¼″ seam allowance. Press the seam allowances open.

3. Press the Little Tile freezer-paper templates (1″ × 1″ squares), shiny side down, diagonally onto the right side of the strip set. Take extra care to make sure that the corners of the freezer-paper templates line up exactly with the seamline on the strip set.

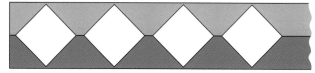

Press templates to strip set.

4. Cut away the fabric precisely along the edge of each freezer-paper template, without adding any extra seam allowances and without cutting into the freezer paper.

5. Peel away the freezer-paper template to reveal the half-square triangle Little Tiles. It is easier to peel away the freezer paper template by holding on to the fabric in the seam allowance.

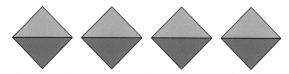

Cut along freezer-paper edge and remove template.

Each 20″-long strip set yields about 13–14 half-square triangle Little Tiles.

> **TIP**
>
> Need a lot of half-square triangle tiles? Get 24–25 Little Tiles or 15–16 Big Tiles from each set by scrimping (see Fabric Scrimping, page 13).

1. Rotary cut a strip of fabric 1½″ × 20″.

2. Mark a line down the length of the strip center using a ruler and pencil.

3. Set your sewing machine for a ⅛″-wide satin stitch. Use a contrasting color thread on top and in the bobbin. Satin stitch over the marked line.

4. Press Little Tile freezer-paper templates (1″ × 1″ square), shiny side down, diagonally onto the right side of the fabric so that the freezer-paper template corners line up exactly with the center of the satin-stitched line.

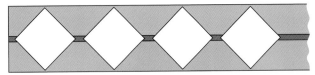

Press templates to strip.

5. Cut away the fabric precisely along the edge of the freezer-paper template without adding any extra seam allowances and without cutting into the freezer paper. Peel away the freezer paper to reveal the tiles. Each 20″-long strip yields about 13–14 satin-stitched stem Little Tiles.

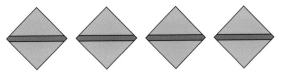

Cut along freezer-paper edge and remove template.

making mini-mosaic big tiles

All the Mini-Mosaic Big Tiles start out measuring 1½″ × 1½″ square from raw edge to raw edge and finish up measuring 1″ × 1″ square after stitching.

Making Plain Big Tiles

Rotary cut strips 1½″ × 20″ and then cut into 1½″ × 1½″ tiles. Each 20″-long strip yields about 12–13 plain Big Tiles.

Making Pieced Big Tiles

MAKING HALF-SQUARE RECTANGLE BIG TILES

Note: Refer to Making Half-Square Rectangle Little Tiles (page 6).

Half-square rectangle Big Tiles require 2 strips 1″ × 20″. Stitch the strips together and then cut the strip set into 1½″ × 1½″ square tiles.

Each strip set yields approximately 12–13 half-square rectangle Big Tiles.

MAKING HALF-SQUARE TRIANGLE BIG TILES

Note: Refer to Making Half-Square Triangle Little Tiles (page 6).

Half-square triangle Big Tiles require 2 strips 1½″ × 20″. Use the Big Tile freezer-paper templates (1½″ × 1½″ square).

Each 20″-long strip set yields about 8–9 half-square triangle Big Tiles.

MAKING QUARTER-SQUARE TRIANGLE BIG TILES

1. Rotary cut 4 strips 1½″ × 20″.

2. Stitch 2 strip sets, each made from 2 strips stitched right sides together, lengthwise, using a ¼″ seam allowance. Press the seam allowances on both sets flat in opposite directions.

3. Rotary cut both strip sets into 1½″-wide segments.

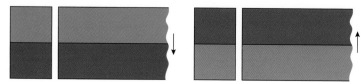

Rotary cut strip sets into segments.

4. Stitch segments into four-patch units, butting up the center seams.

Press the center seam allowances on the four-patch units open.

Stitch segments into four-patch units.

5. Press Big Tile freezer-paper templates (1½″ × 1½″ square), shiny side down, diagonally, onto the right side of the four-patch unit, taking extra care to make sure the 4 corners of the freezer-paper templates line up exactly with the four-patch seamlines.

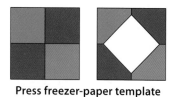

Press freezer-paper template onto four-patch unit.

6. Cut away the fabric precisely along the edge of the template, without adding any extra seam allowances and without cutting into the freezer paper. Peel away the freezer-paper template to reveal the quarter-square triangle Big Tiles.

Cut along freezer-paper edge and remove templates.

Each 20″-long strip set yields about 12–13 of the 1½″-wide segments.

MAKING HALF- AND QUARTER-SQUARE TRIANGLE BIG TILES

1. Rotary cut 2 strips 1½″ × 20″.

2. Stitch the strips right sides together, lengthwise, using a ¼″ seam allowance. Press the seam allowances of the strip set open.

3. Rotary cut the set into 1½″-wide segments.

4. Rotary cut a third fabric into 1 strip 1½″ × 20″.

5. Stitch the segments from Step 3 onto the strip from Step 4, right sides together, using a ¼″ seam allowance. Cut into units and press the seam allowances open.

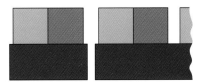

**Chainstitch segments onto fabric strip;
cut into units.**

6. Press the Big Tile freezer-paper templates (1½″ × 1½″ square), shiny side down, diagonally, onto the right side of the fabric units. Take extra care to make sure 3 of the freezer-paper template corners line up exactly with the seamlines.

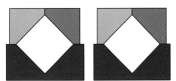

**Press freezer-paper templates
onto fabric units.**

7. Cut away the fabric precisely along the edge of the template, without adding any seam allowance and without cutting into the freezer paper. Peel away the freezer-paper template to reveal the half- and quarter-square triangle Big Tiles.

**Cut along freezer paper edge
and remove templates.**

Each 20″-long set of the first 2 fabrics yields about 12–13 of the 1½″-wide segments, which then require about 2 strips 20″ long of the third fabric to create 13 complete units.

> **TIP**
>
> Need a lot of half- and quarter-square triangle Big Tiles? Get 14–15 tiles from each fabric set by scrimping (see Fabric Scrimping, page 13).

MAKING CORNER TRIANGLE BIG TILES

1. Rotary cut a strip 1¾″ × 20″ for the large, miter-shaped part of the tile and a strip 1″ × 20″ for the small, triangular corner part of the tile.

2. Stitch the strips to each other, right sides together, using a scant ¼″ seam allowance. Press the seam allowances open.

3. Cut a 1½″ × 1½″ square of ¼″ gridded template plastic and mark as shown on the diagram.

4. Cut away the small triangle from the plastic template.

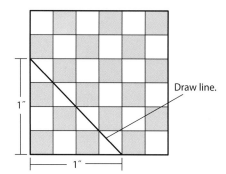

Mark and cut plastic template.

5. Use the miter-shaped plastic template to mark and draw a line across 1½″ × 1½″ freezer-paper plain Big Tile templates.

6. Press the marked freezer-paper templates onto the prepared fabric set, shiny side down, lining up the drawn line on the freezer paper with the seamline.

**Press marked freezer-paper
templates onto strip set.**

7. Cut around the edge of the freezer-paper template without adding any extra seam allowances and without cutting into the freezer paper; then peel off the freezer paper to reveal the corner triangle Big Tiles.

**Cut along freezer-paper edge
and remove templates.**

Each 20″ strip set yields about 8–9 corner triangle Big Tiles.

8. Or, for double corner triangle Big Tiles, rotary cut both of the strips 1¾″ × 20″.

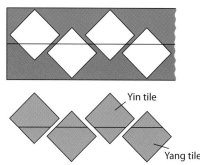

Making double corner triangle Big Tiles

Each 20″ strip set will yield about 11–12 double corner triangle Big Tiles.

> **TIP**
>
> Need a lot of corner triangle Big Tiles? Get 12 yin and 12 yang (above) from each fabric set by scrimping. (See Fabric Scrimping, page 13, and remember that there are essentially 3 rows of staggered cut squares.)

MAKING FOUR-PATCH BIG TILES

1. Rotary cut 4 strips 1˝ × 20˝.

2. Stitch the strips lengthwise into 2 sets, Set A and Set B, of 2 strips each, right sides together, using a ¼˝ seam allowance. Press the seam allowances flat in opposite directions on each of the sets.

3. Rotary cut each set into 1˝-wide segments (each set yields 19–20 segments).

4. Stitch together segments of Sets A and B, aligning the center seams and using a ¼˝ seam allowance. Press the seam allowances open to complete the four-patch Big Tiles, each measuring 1½˝ × 1½˝.

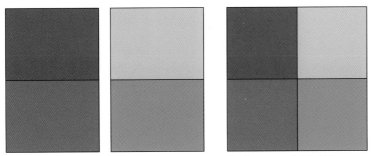

Stitch segments A and B together to make four-patch Big Tiles.

MAKING HALF-SQUARE TRAPEZOID BIG TILES

1. Rotary cut 2 strips 1½˝ × 20˝.

2. Stitch the strips, right sides together, using a ¼˝ seam allowance. Press the seam allowances open.

3. Cut a 1½˝ × 1½˝ square of ¼˝ gridded template plastic and mark it as shown. Cut the plastic template on the marked line.

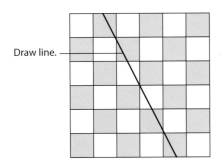

Draw line.

Mark and cut template plastic.

4. Cut out plain Big Tile freezer-paper templates. Use the plastic trapezoid to draw a line across the freezer-paper templates.

5. Press the marked freezer-paper templates onto the prepared fabric set, aligning the drawn line with the seamline.

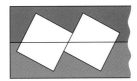

Press marked freezer-paper templates onto strip set.

6. Cut around the freezer-paper template edge without adding any extra seam allowances and without cutting into the freezer paper. Then peel off the template to reveal the half-square trapezoid Big Tiles. Each 20˝-long strip set yields about 9–10 half-square trapezoid Big Tiles.

Cut along freezer-paper edge and remove templates.

TIP

Need a lot of half-square trapezoid Big Tiles? Get 20 tiles from each fabric set by scrimping (see Fabric Scrimping, page 13).

MAKING STEM BIG TILES

1. Rotary cut 2 strips 1½″ × 20″ and a strip ¾″ × 20″.

2. Stitch the strips lengthwise, right sides together, using a ¼″ seam allowance, with the narrow ¾″-wide strip between the 2 wider strips. Press the seam allowances away from the narrow strip.

3. Press Big Tile freezer-paper templates (1½″ × 1½″ square), shiny side down, diagonally, onto the right side of the fabric set. The corners of the freezer-paper templates line up with the center of the narrow ¼″-wide strip.

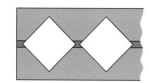

Center and press freezer-paper
templates onto strip set.

4. Cut away the fabric precisely along the edge of the template, without adding any extra seam allowances and without cutting into the freezer paper. Peel away the freezer-paper template to reveal the stem Big Tiles.

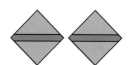

Cut along freezer-paper edge
and remove templates.

Each 20″-long strip set yields about 8–9 stem Big Tiles.

TIP

Need a lot of stem Big Tiles? Get 16–17 tiles from each fabric set by scrimping (see Fabric Scrimping, page 13).

MAKING STEM-AND-TRIANGLE BIG TILES

1. Rotary cut 2 strips 1½″ × 20″ and a strip ¾″ × 20″.

2. Stitch the strips, right sides together, lengthwise, using a ¼″ seam allowance, with the narrow ¾″-wide strip between the 2 wider strips. Press the seam allowances away from the narrow strip.

3. Rotary cut the strip set into stem segments 1½″ wide.

Cut set into segments.

4. Rotary cut another strip 1½″ × 20″.

5. Stitch the stem segments onto the fabric strip, right sides together, using a ¼″ seam allowance. Press the seam allowances open.

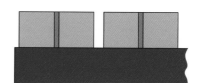

Stitch stem segments onto fabric strip.

6. Press Big Tile freezer-paper templates (1½″ × 1½″ square), shiny side down, diagonally, onto the right side of the strip set. The diagonal corners of the freezer-paper templates line up with the last seam, with a third point of the template lining up with center of the narrow ¼″-wide strip.

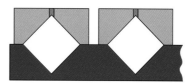

Center and press freezer-paper
templates onto strip set.

7. Cut away the fabric precisely along the edge of the freezer-paper template. Peel away the freezer-paper template to reveal the stem-and-triangle Big Tiles.

Cut along freezer-paper edge and remove templates.

Each 20″-long strip set yields about 6–7 stem-and-triangle Big Tiles.

TIP

Need a lot of stem-and-triangle Big Tiles? Get 12–13 tiles stacked on both sides of a long 20″ strip by scrimping (see Fabric Scrimping, at right).

fabric scrimping

Making a lot of tiles for your Mini-Mosaic projects? Fabric scrimping is a way to use up most of the fabric that is trimmed away when making half-square triangle Little Tiles and some Big Tiles. Follow this procedure.

1. Cut the fabric strips wider than stated in the previous tile instructions (see Fabric Scrimping Cutting and Yield chart, page 14). For example, for half-square triangle Big Tiles, cut the strips 2″ wide instead of 1½″ wide.

2. When cutting out the tiles, don't cut the individual tiles apart from each other. Start cutting at a center seam and around half the templates, keeping them all in a row. When you get to the end of the row you will have 2 jagged-edged pieces of fabric.

3. Stitch the remaining straight edges of the strip, right sides together, using a ¼″ seam allowance. Press the seam allowance open.

4. Press the additional Big Tile freezer-paper templates in place over the new seam, making sure that the template corners line up exactly with the seamline. Use scissors to cut templates apart and trim away the excess fabric around the template. Peel away the freezer-paper templates to reveal the tiles.

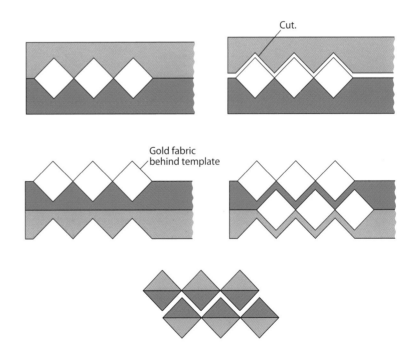

Fabric scrimping on half-square triangle tiles

The example shown is for half-square triangle tiles, but the same basic fabric scrimping principles apply to all the listed tiles. For stem Big Tiles inset an additional ¾"-wide rotary-cut strip of contrasting fabric into the new seam. Don't increase the width of these contrast strips when scrimping.

For half- and quarter-square triangle Big Tiles and stem-and-triangle Big Tiles, make additional "striped" segments and add them to the other side of the ½"-wider cut fabric strip, offsetting them half a tile's width. Don't increase the widths of the "striped" portion; just increase the width of the long strip when scrimping.

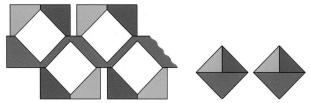

Fabric scrimping on half- and quarter-square triangle Big Tiles

Fabric Scrimping Cutting and Yield

TILE TYPE		CUT STRIP WIDTH	TILE YIELD PER 20″ STRIP
LITTLE TILES	Half-square triangle	1½″	24–25
BIG TILES	Half-square triangle	2″	15–16
	Half- and quarter-square triangle	Cut center strip 2″ wide; cut other strips as before (page 9)	14–15
	Corner triangle	3″	12 yin and 12 yang (page 10)
	Half-square trapezoid	2½″	20
	Stem	2 background strips 1¾″ and 2 stem strips ¾″	16–17
	Stem-and-triangle	Cut center strip 2″ wide; cut other strips as before (page 12)	12–13

making tile blanks for individual tiles

What if you're only making a few of each tile type and you don't really need a full 20″-long strip of fabric? Then it makes sense to cut the strips into smaller segments that you can use to make individual blanks for the pieced tiles. This technique is especially useful when making the individual blocks, such as those in *Tesserae Sampler Quilt* (page 53), which calls for a lot of different tiles but not very many of each.

For Little Tiles, this technique would apply only when making the half-square triangle tiles. Cut segments 1″ × 2″ of the fabrics being used and stitch 2 of the segments together lengthwise. Press the seam allowance open and press on a Little Tile 1″ × 1″ freezer-paper template. Then cut out the individual tile.

For Big Tiles, cut segments from the 1½″-wide strips into square segments 1½″ × 1½″ and rectangular segments 2½″ × 1½″, and make the tile blanks.

For example, when making the blanks for half-square triangle Big Tiles, use 2 of the rectangle segments. When making a blank for a quarter-square triangle Big Tile, use 4 of the square segments, and when making a blank for a half- and quarter-square triangle Big Tile, use 2 square segments and 1 rectangle segment, and so on.

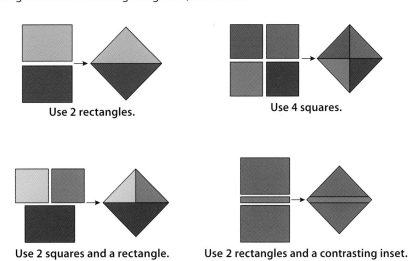

Use 2 rectangles.

Use 4 squares.

Use 2 squares and a rectangle.

Use 2 rectangles and a contrasting inset.

Making individual Big Tiles from blanks

 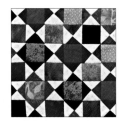   

making the
MINI-MOSAIC

using the grid sheets

Just as there are two tile sizes, there are two Mini-Mosaic layout grids, the Little Tile Layout Grid and the Big Tile Layout Grid. These grids are found on pullout pages P1 and P2. These reusable layout grids have been designed so that the internal measurement of each square is 1″ × 1″ on the Little Tile Layout Grid, or 1½″ × 1½″ on the Big Tile Layout Grid, exclusive of the thickness of the line that separates the squares. For example, if you were to measure across six squares 1″ × 1″ on the Little Tile layout grid, you would find that the measurement is slightly more than 6″. The extra line thickness between the squares will make it easy to position the tiles without any overlapping, which makes it easy to fold and stitch. To use the Tile Layout Grid sheets, simply place the appropriate grid, right side up, onto an ironing surface and overlay with a piece of interfacing, onto which the Mini-Mosaic tiles will be fused.

fusing the
mini-mosaic tiles

1. Place the appropriate Tile Layout Grid sheet, right side up, onto an ironing surface.

Note: June Tailor Quilter's Cut 'n Press III, with an ironing surface just slightly larger than the full-sized grid sheet, is ideal for Mini-Mosaics.

> **TIP**
>
> Rather than using the printed grid sheets, you can carefully trace the grid lines onto a piece of muslin using a permanent pen. You may find the muslin easier to work with.

2. Cut a piece of lightweight fusible interfacing just larger than called for by the pattern, and place it, fusible side up, over the grid. The grid should be fully visible through the interfacing. Pin both the interfacing and the grid sheet onto the ironing surface.

3. Position the first row of fabric tiles, right side up, onto the interfacing according to the placement diagram for the Mini-Mosaic pattern. Make sure that each fabric tile rests on the interfacing fully within the outline of a square of the Tile Layout Grid beneath. For example, here is the placement diagram for the Tenley's Teatime Tango block, which shows the position for each of the 25 tiles that go into making it.

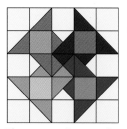

**Placement diagram for
Tenley's Teatime Tango**

4. Touch each fabric tile with the heated tip of an iron or mini-iron to adhere it to the interfacing, making sure each tile is positioned as squarely as possible over a grid square. This is only the first stage of the fusing process, so don't worry too much if every bit of the tile isn't fused completely to the interfacing. Don't use steam at this stage because the paper grid may curl. Fuse a row of tiles at a time, taking care to position the tile precisely as in the placement diagram. Continue the fusing process until the pattern is complete.

Initial fusing of tiles

TIP

If you make a mistake, such as turning a pieced tile the wrong way around or slightly askew, simply reheat the tile with the iron and lift it off immediately, while it is still hot. The tile can then be repositioned and re-ironed in place.

5. Finish fusing the tiles after checking to make sure all of them are in the correct places according to the placement diagram.

Trim away the excess interfacing around the edge of the Mini-Mosaic. Turn the piece wrong side up onto the ironing surface.

Cover with a pressing cloth and press with a hot iron (following interfacing manufacturer's directions) until all tiles are fully and securely fused in place on the interfacing.

Note: Adjacent tiles should almost, but not quite, touch each other. Use a silicon release paper as a pressing cloth to prevent the fusible interfacing from sticking to your iron.

stitching and pressing seams

All of the Mini-Mosaic stitching is done by machine, using a small straight stitch (set the stitch length at 2 or 2.5mm) and a ¼″ presser foot. The prepared fused Mini-Mosaic panels or blocks are simply folded, right sides together, along the line between the tiles, and then stitched ¼″ away from the fold.

1. When stitching, alternate sewing directions of adjacent seams to help keep the Mini-Mosaic straight.

Fold and stitch Mini-Mosaic panel.

2. Clip through the interfacing fold with a small, sharp-pointed pair of scissors so that the seam allowances can be opened for the whole length of the seam.

Cut through interfacing after stitching parallel seams.

3. Press the seam allowances open.

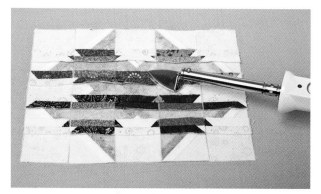

Press seam allowances open.

4. Repeat Steps 1–3 to fold and stitch all of the seam allowances in the perpendicular direction, clip the interfacing, and press the seam allowances open. Your Mini-Mosaic unit is complete!

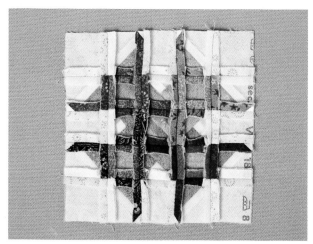

Back side of finished block

Front side of finished block

quilting mini-mosaics

After the Mini-Mosaic block or panel is complete, it is ready to include in a quilt or quilted project. Layer the quilt top with batting and backing, and baste the three layers together. Mini-Mosaics don't need a lot of quilting. Here the Tenley's Teatime Tango block has been incorporated into a small quilted notebook cover. This piece uses cotton flannel instead of batting, and the quilting is limited to a bit of free-motion stipple quilting done with a light-colored silk thread in the cream fabric areas of the block.

Mini-Mosaics are easy to machine quilt.

This sample of the Friendship Star Chain pattern has been quilted with simple straight lines through the chain using a walking foot, again using a thin batting and silk thread.

Simple diagonal quilting is all that's needed.

binding

Trim to square up the quilt and ensure all layers are even. The number of strips to cut for binding and their width is given in each project. Use your favorite method to join binding strips and bind the project.

rosebud row
PLACEMAT

FINISHED SIZE: 14″ × 11″

materials and cutting

Instructions are for making one placemat, but you will have enough fabric to make two. Refer to Cutting Fabric Strips (page 5).

COLOR AND USE	YARDAGE	CUTTING
FABRIC 1: Outer rosebud	1 fat quarter	Cut 3 strips 1″ × 20″; then cut into 54 plain Little Tiles (1″ × 1″).
FABRIC 2: Inner rosebud, binding	1 fat quarter	Cut 1 strip 1″ × 20″; then cut into 18 plain Little Tiles (1″ × 1″). Cut 4 strips 1½″ × 20″ for binding.
FABRIC 3: Leaves	1 fat quarter	Cut 2 strips 1″ × 20″; then cut into 36 plain Little Tiles (1″ × 1″).
FABRIC 4: Chain	1 fat quarter	Cut 3 strips 1″ × 20″; then cut into 51 plain Little Tiles (1″ × 1″).
FABRIC 5: Background, inner border	2 fat quarters	Cut 7 strips 1″ × 20″; then cut into 138 plain Little Tiles (1″ × 1″) for background. Cut 2 strips 1½″ × 20″ and make 18 satin-stitched stem Little Tiles (page 7). Cut 2 strips 1″ × 20″ for inner border.
FABRIC 6:* Outer border, backing	3 fat quarters	Cut 4 strips 1¾″ × 20″ for outer border. Cut 1 piece 13″ × 16″ for backing.

* For Fabric 6, consider using a print fabric that includes one or more colors from the other selected fabrics.

you will also need:

- Little Tile freezer-paper templates (see Cutting Freezer-Paper Tile Templates, page 6): 18 templates 1″ × 1″

- Thin batting or flannel: 1 piece 12″ × 15″

- Lightweight fusible interfacing: 1 piece 20″ × 26″

- Thread to match the color of Fabric 3 for stems

MAKE THE PLACEMAT

Seam allowances are ¼″ unless otherwise noted.

1. Make the plain Little Tiles (page 6).

Make the satin-stitched stem Little Tiles (page 7).

Make 54.

Make 18.

Make 36.

Make 51.

Make 138.

Make 18.

**Rosebud Row Placemat
Mini-Mosaic tiles**

2. Arrange the tiles according to the placement diagram (at right) and fuse them in place. Sew to make the Mini-Mosaic center panel for the placemat (page 17). Press.

The panel measures 8″ × 11″ when sewn. Use a rotary cutter and a ruler to straighten the edges of the quilt top if needed.

3. Cut each of the inner border strips into 2 pieces 1″ × 11″ and 1″ × 9″. Sew the longer inner border strips to the top and bottom edges of the center panel and then sew the remaining inner border strips to the side edges. Press as you go.

4. Cut the outer border strips into 2 pieces 1¾″ × 11½″ and 2 pieces 1¾″ × 12″. Sew the longer pieces to the top and bottom edges of the center panel and then sew the remaining pieces to the side edges. Press as you go.

5. Referring to Quilting Mini-Mosaics (page 18), sandwich the placemat top with the thin batting or flannel and the backing; baste and quilt as desired.

6. Join the binding strips and bind using your favorite method (see Binding, page 18).

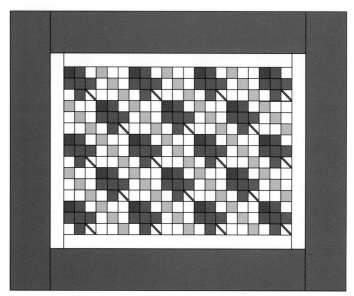
Rosebud Row block placement diagram

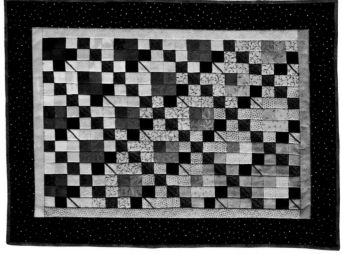
Scrappy version of Rosebud Row Placemat

friendship star chain
TABLE RUNNER

FINISHED SIZE: 19″ × 79″

materials and cutting

Refer to Cutting Fabric Strips (page 5).

COLOR AND USE	YARDAGE	CUTTING
FABRIC 1: Blocks and sashing	2 fat quarters	Cut 5 strips 1″ × 20″; then cut into 100 plain Little Tiles (1″ × 1″). Cut 10 strips 1½″ × 20″; then cut into 20 pieces 1½″ × 9″ for sashing.
FABRIC 2: Blocks	1 fat eighth	Cut 4 strips 1″ × 20″; then cut into 80 plain Little Tiles (1″ × 1″).
FABRIC 3: Blocks, sashing posts, and outer border corners	1 fat quarter	Cut 6 strips 1″ × 20″; then cut into 120 plain Little Tiles (1″ × 1″). Cut 2 strips 1½″ × 20″; then cut into 20 squares 1½″ × 1½″ for sashing posts. Cut 1 strip 2½″ × 20″; then cut into 4 squares 2½″ × 2½″ for border corners.
FABRIC 4: Blocks	1 fat eighth	Cut 5 strips 1″ × 20″; then cut into 100 plain Little Tiles (1″ × 1″).
FABRIC 5: Blocks and binding	⅝ yard	Cut 3 strips 1″ × 20″; then cut into 50 plain Little Tiles (1″ × 1″). Cut 2 strips 1½″ × 20″ for half-square triangle Little Tiles. Cut 6 strips 2½″ × width of fabric for binding.
FABRIC 6: Blocks	1 fat eighth	Cut 4 strips 1″ × 20″; then cut into 75 plain Little Tiles (1″ × 1″). Cut 2 strips 1½″ × 20″ for half-square triangle Little Tiles.
FABRIC 7: Blocks	1 fat eighth	Cut 3 strips 1″ × 20″; then cut into 50 plain Little Tiles (1″ × 1″). Cut 2 strips 1½″ × 20″ for half-square triangle Little Tiles.
FABRIC 8: Blocks and outer border	⅝ yard	Cut 3 strips 1″ × 20″; then cut into 50 plain Little Tiles (1″ × 1″). Cut 2 strips 1½″ × 20″ for half-square triangle Little Tiles. Cut 5 strips 2½″ × 40″ for outer border.
FABRIC 9: Background fabric and block inner borders	3 fat quarters	Cut 21 strips 1″ × 20″; then cut into 420 plain Little Tiles (1″ × 1″). Cut 8 strips 1½″ × 20″ for half-square triangle Little Tiles. Cut 10 strips 1″ × 20″ for inner borders; then cut into 10 pieces 8″ long and 10 pieces 9″ long.
FABRIC 10: Setting triangles	⅞ yard	Cut 2 squares 8⅜″ × 8⅜″; then cut each in half on the diagonal for 4 corner setting triangles. Cut 2 squares 16¼″ × 16¼″; then cut in quarters diagonally for 8 side setting triangles.

you will also need:

- Little Tile freezer-paper templates (see Cutting Freezer-Paper Tile Templates, page 6): 80 templates 1″ × 1″

- Thin batting or flannel: 1 piece 25″ × 83″

- Lightweight fusible interfacing: 5 pieces 17″ × 17″

- Backing fabric: 25″ × 83″

MAKE THE TABLE RUNNER

Seam allowances are ¼″ unless otherwise noted. Instructions for making the 5 blocks with inner borders and sashing posts are simplified for ease of construction. Each block has its own set of 4 gold sashing posts (see the runner assembly diagram, page 24).

1. Make the plain Little Tiles (page 6).

Make the half-square triangle Little Tiles (page 6). Use fabric scrimping (page 13).

Make 100. Make 80. Make 120. Make 100. Make 50. Make 75. Make 50.

Make 50. Make 420. Make 20. Make 20. Make 20. Make 20.

Friendship Star Chain Mini-Mosaic tiles

2. Make 5 Friendship Star Chain Mini-Mosaic blocks as shown. Press.

Friendship Star Chain block placement diagram

3. Stitch the inner borders onto the blocks. Press as you go.
The blocks measure 9″ × 9″.

4. Add the block side sashing strips. Press. Sew the corner posts onto the top and bottom block sashing strips. Press. Add these sashing strips to the top and bottom of the block. Press. The blocks now measure 11″ × 11″. Rotate the blocks as you like.

Add inner block borders and sashing.

Like this pattern? Make bigger version for cushion cover or wallhanging.

5. Stitch the setting triangles to the blocks. Press. The table runner now measures approximately 15¼″ × 74¾″.

6. Stitch together 4 of the 2½″-wide outer border strips to make 2 long pieces about 80″ long. Press. From these, cut 2 borders 74¾″ long (or to match the length of your table runner), and stitch them to the long sides of the table runner. Press. Cut the remaining 2½″-wide strip into 2 pieces 15¼″ long (or to match the width of your runner). Stitch a 2½″ × 2½″ border corner square to each end of the strips; then stitch these strips to the short sides of the table runner. Press.

7. Referring to Quilting Mini-Mosaics (page 18), sandwich the table runner layers; baste and quilt as desired.

8. Join the binding strips and bind using your favorite method (see Binding, page 18).

Runner assembly diagram

rambling rose
HANDBAG

FINISHED SIZE: approximately
16½″ wide × 11½″ high × 5″ deep

materials and cutting

Refer to Cutting Fabric Strips (page 5).

COLOR AND USE	YARDAGE	CUTTING
FABRIC 1: Background	1 fat quarter	Cut 9 strips 1″ × 20″; then cut into 174 plain Little Tiles (1″ × 1″). Cut 4 strips 1½″ × 20″ for half-square triangle Little Tiles.
FABRIC 2: Background	1 fat quarter	Cut 11 strips 1″ × 20″; then cut into 210 plain Little Tiles (1″ × 1″). Cut 4 strips 1½″ × 20″ for half-square triangle Little Tiles.
FABRIC 3: Rose	1 fat eighth	Cut 4 strips 1″ × 20″; then cut into 72 plain Little Tiles (1″ × 1″).
FABRIC 4: Rose	1 fat eighth	Cut 4 strips 1½″ × 20″ for half-square triangle Little Tiles.
FABRIC 5: Center of rose	1 fat eighth	Cut 1 strip 1″ × 20″; then cut into 18 plain Little Tiles (1″ × 1″).
FABRIC 6: Leaves and vines	1 fat quarter	Cut 3 strips 1″ × 20″; then cut into 42 plain Little Tiles (1″ × 1″). Cut 8 strips 1½″ × 20″ for half-square triangle Little Tiles.
FABRIC 7: Checkerboard	1 fat eighth	Cut 4 strips 1″ × 20″; then cut into 78 plain Little Tiles (1″ × 1″).
FABRIC 8: Checkerboard	1 fat eighth	Cut 4 strips 1″ × 20″; then cut into 78 plain Little Tiles (1″ × 1″).
FABRIC 9: Trim, handle straps, and ties	¾ yard	Cut 1 strip 2″ × width of fabric (40″–42″) for bag top trim. Cut 1 strip 6½″ × width of fabric for bag outer bottom. Cut 2 strips 4¼″ × width of fabric for bag straps. Cut 3 strips 1¼″ × width of fabric for side ties and key loop.
FABRIC 10: Lining	½ yard	Cut 1 strip 14½″ × width of fabric for bag lining.
FABRIC 11: Pockets and bag bottom	¾ yard	Cut 1 strip 11″ × width of fabric for interior pockets. Cut 1 piece 9½″ × 12″ to cover bag bottom insert.

you will also need:

- Little Tile freezer-paper templates (see Cutting Freezer-Paper Tile Templates, page 6): 186 templates 1″ × 1″

- Lightweight fusible interfacing: 1 piece 15″ × 70″

- Fusible fleece, 1¼ yards, cut into these pieces:
  2 pieces 14″ × 42″
  1 piece 5″ × 42″

- Heavyweight fusible interfacing: 2 pieces 3″ × 33″

- Plastic canvas:
  1 piece 4½″ × 11″

- Foam core board: 1 piece 10mm thick or 2 pieces 5mm thick, cut 4″ × 10½″ for bag bottom insert (you can also use several layers of mat board or heavy interfacing)

- Protective bag feet: 4 large (the type with "wings" that open flat)

- D-rings: 4 pieces 1½″ (or 4 flat rectangle rings 1½″)

- Button: 1 large, 1½″–2½″ diameter

- Batting remnant: approximately 9″ × 11″

- Template plastic: 1 piece cut 2½″ × 2½″

- Bolt snap or key ring: 1 (optional)

- Pandora-style glass charm beads: 4 pieces, with 2mm bore holes (optional)

MAKE THE BAG

Seam allowances are ¼″ unless otherwise noted.

1. Make the plain Little Tiles (page 6).

2. Make the half-square triangle Little Tiles (page 6).

Stitch the 1½″ × 20″ strips together to make 4 sets of Fabrics 1 and 6, 2 sets of Fabrics 2 and 6, 2 sets of Fabrics 4 and 6, and 2 sets of Fabrics 2 and 4.

> **TIP**
> Use fabric scrimping (see page 13) when making all half-square triangle Little Tiles.

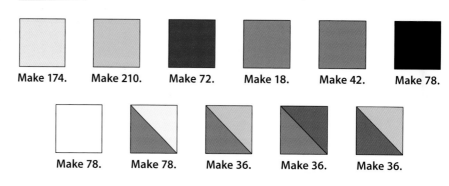

Make 174. Make 210. Make 72. Make 18. Make 42. Make 78.

Make 78. Make 78. Make 36. Make 36. Make 36.

Rambling Rose Mini-Mosaic tiles

3. Starting on the left side, fuse the tiles to the 15″ × 70″ piece of fusible interfacing according to the placement diagram (below) for a single pattern repeat.

4. Repeat the tile block pattern 5 more times; then stitch to finish.

Single pattern repeat

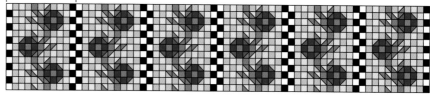

Rambling Rose block placement diagram

> **TIP**
> The Rambling Rose panel measures 7″ × 33½″. The finished size of your panel may vary slightly, so measure your panel and use your measurement wherever the pattern states 33½″, adjusting other measurements as needed.

RAMBLING ROSE HANDBAG is continued on page 64.

zigzag
WALLET

FINISHED SIZE: 7″ × 10½″ open flat

materials and cutting

Refer to Cutting Fabric Strips (page 5).

COLOR AND USE	YARDAGE	CUTTING
FABRIC 1: Bright red for blocks, coin purse, and pocket lining	1 fat quarter	Cut 3 strips 1″ × 20″; then cut into 60 plain Little Tiles (1″ × 1″). Cut 1 piece 7½″ × 8″ for coin purse. Cut 1 piece 5″ × 7½″ for pocket lining.
FABRIC 2: Orange/red for blocks and coin purse flap	1 fat quarter	Cut 6 strips 1½″ × 20″ for half-square triangle Little Tiles. Cut 2 pieces 4″ × 7½″ for coin purse flap.
FABRIC 3: Lime green for blocks, wallet lining, pocket lining, and ID card section	½ yard full width (40″)	Cut 1 strip 3½″ × 40″ (width of fabric) for ID card section. Cut 3 strips 1½″ × 20″ for half-square triangle Little Tiles. Cut 1 piece 7″ × 11″ for wallet lining.
FABRIC 4: Medium/dark green for blocks	1 fat quarter	Cut 3 strips 1½″ × 20″ for half-square triangle Little Tiles.
FABRIC 5: Dark green for blocks and binding	2 fat quarters	Cut 1 piece 15″ × 15″ for bias binding. Cut 6 strips 1½″ × 20″ for half-square triangle Little Tiles.

you will also need:

- Little Tile freezer-paper templates (see Cutting Freezer-Paper Tile Templates, page 6): Start with 60 templates 1″ × 1″ and reuse templates. Cut more if needed.

- Lightweight fusible interfacing: 1 piece 14″ × 22″

- Batting or fusible fleece: 1 piece 7″ × 11″, 2 pieces 3¾″ × 7″

- Quilter's Vinyl (by C&T Publishing): 3½″ × 4½″ piece for ID card section insert

- Sew-in hook and loop tape: 2 small pieces 1″

- Decorative buttons or small yo-yos to hide sew-in stitching: 2 pieces 1¼″ (optional)

MAKE THE WALLET

Seam allowances are ¼″ unless otherwise noted.

1. Make the plain Little Tiles (page 6) using Fabric 1.

Make the half-square triangle Little Tiles (page 6). Stitch 3 sets each of Fabrics 2 and 3, Fabrics 2 and 5, and Fabrics 4 and 5. Use fabric scrimping (page 13).

Make 60.

Make 60.

Make 60.

Make 60.

Zigzag Wallet Little Tiles

2. Make the Zigzag Mini-Mosaic panel according to the placement diagram. The panel measures 6½″ × 10½″ when sewn.

Zigzag block placement diagram

ZIGZAG WALLET is continued on page 66.

tess the starlet block and
SEWING BOX

FINISHED SIZE: 13″ wide × 13″ long × 5″ deep

materials and cutting

Refer to Cutting Fabric Strips (page 5).

COLOR AND USE	YARDAGE	CUTTING
FABRIC 1	1 fat eighth	Cut 2 strips 1″ × 20″; then cut into 27–28 plain Little Tiles (1″ × 1″). Cut 1 strip 1½″ × 20″ for half-square triangle Little Tiles.
FABRIC 2	1 fat eighth	Cut 2 strips 1″ × 20″; then cut into 27–28 plain Little Tiles (1″ × 1″). Cut 1 strip 1½″ × 20″ for half-square triangle Little Tiles.
FABRIC 3	1 fat eighth	Cut 1 strip 1″ × 20″; then cut into 18–19 plain Little Tiles (1″ × 1″). Cut 2 strips 1½″ × 20″ for half-square triangle Little Tiles.
FABRIC 4	1 fat eighth	Cut 1 strip 1″ × 20″; then cut into 18–19 plain Little Tiles (1″ × 1″). Cut 2 strips 1½″ × 20″ for half-square triangle Little Tiles.
FABRIC 5	1 fat eighth	Cut 2 strips 1″ × 20″; then cut into 27–28 plain Little Tiles (1″ × 1″). Cut 1 strip 1½″ × 20″ for half-square triangle Little Tiles.
FABRIC 6	1 fat eighth	Cut 2 strips 1″ × 20″; then cut into 27–28 plain Little Tiles (1″ × 1″). Cut 1 strip 1½″ × 20″ for half-square triangle Little Tiles.
FABRIC 7	1 fat eighth	Cut 1 strip 1″ × 20″; then cut into 18–19 plain Little Tiles (1″ × 1″). Cut 2 strips 1½″ × 20″ for half-square triangle Little Tiles.
FABRIC 8	1 fat eighth	Cut 1 strip 1″ × 20″; then cut into 18–19 plain Little Tiles (1″ × 1″). Cut 2 strips 1½″ × 20″ for half-square triangle Little Tiles.
FABRIC 9	1 fat quarter	Cut 6 strips 1″ × 20″; then cut into 108 plain Little Tiles (1″ × 1″). Cut 4 strips 1½″ × 20″ for half-square triangle Little Tiles.
FABRIC 10: 40″ width of fabric for border around Mini-Mosaic, box sides, and box bottom	1 yard	Cut 1 strip 15″ × width of fabric; then cut into 1 square 15″ × 15″ for box bottom, and into 2 pieces 3″ × 10½″ and 2 pieces 3″ × 15½″ for border on box top. Cut 2 strips 7″ × width of fabric and stitch together lengthwise to cover outer sides of box. Cut 3 pieces 2″ × 4″ for hinges. Cut 1 strip 1½″ × width of fabric; then cut into 4 pieces 1½″ × 9″ for button loops.
FABRIC 11: 40″ width of fabric for box lining and internal pockets	1⅛ yard	Cut 1 strip 15″ × width of fabric; then cut into 2 squares 15″ × 15″ for lining box top and inner box bottom. Cut 2 strips 7″ × width of fabric; then cut into 4 pieces 7″ × 15″ for lining inner box sides. Cut 1 strip 6″ × width of fabric; then cut into 2 pieces 6″ × 18″ for interior side pockets.

you will also need:

- Little Tile freezer-paper templates (see Cutting Freezer-Paper Tile Templates, page 6): 112 templates 1″ × 1″

- Lightweight fusible interfacing: 1 piece 22″ × 22″

- Batting, about 30″ × 60″ low-loft polyester or similar, cut into these pieces:

  1 piece 6″ × 54″

  4 pieces 6″ × 14″

  4 pieces 14″ × 14″

- Mat board (4 or 6 ply) or grey board (available in Europe), 3 sheets, rotary cut into these pieces:

  1 piece 13″ × 13″ for exterior of box top

  1 piece 12¾″ × 12¾″ for bottom exterior of box

  2 pieces 12½″ × 12½″ for interior lining of box top and box bottom

  4 pieces 5″ × 12¾″ for exterior box sides

  4 pieces 4¾″ × 12½″ for interior box sides lining

- Strong PVA glue and glue spreader

- Elastic: 2½ yards ¼″ wide

- Clothespins or large bulldog clips

- Curved needle

- Hand quilting thread in the same color as Fabric 10

- Shank buttons (*optional*) for box closure: 4 large 1″–1½″

MAKE THE SEWING BOX

Seam allowances are ¼″ unless otherwise noted.

1. Make the plain Little Tiles (page 6).

Make the half-square triangle Little Tiles (page 6). Use fabric scrimping (page 13).

Use the 1½″ strips to piece 1 set each of Fabrics 3 and 9, Fabrics 4 and 9, Fabrics 7 and 9, and Fabrics 8 and 9. Then make 1 set each of Fabrics 1 and 3, Fabrics 2 and 4, Fabrics 5 and 7, and Fabrics 6 and 8.

Use the sets to make the required tiles.

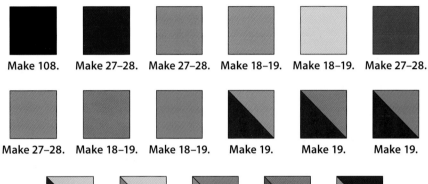

Make 108.   Make 27–28.   Make 27–28.   Make 18–19.   Make 18–19.   Make 27–28.

Make 27–28.   Make 18–19.   Make 18–19.   Make 19.   Make 19.   Make 19.

Make 19.   Make 9.   Make 9.   Make 9.   Make 9.

Little Tiles for Tess the Starlet Sewing Box

2. Make the Tess the Starlet Mini-Mosaic panel according to the layout diagram (at right). The panel measures 10½″ × 10½″ from raw edge to raw edge (10″ × 10″ finished size). In general, I grouped colored pairs of lights/darks together, adding a light/black half-square triangle unit in each corner of the border. There are a few extra plain squares so you can place the colors as you like next to the corners. Each border requires 18 squares between the corners.

Tess the Starlet block placement diagram

TESS THE STARLET SEWING BOX
is continued on page 68.

darting birds
NECK ROLL CUSHION

FINISHED SIZE: approximately 18″ long × 7½″ diameter

materials and cutting

Refer to Cutting Fabric Strips (page 5).

COLOR AND USE	YARDAGE	CUTTING
■ FABRIC 1	2 fat quarters	Cut 16 strips 1″ × 20″; then cut into 304 plain Little Tiles (1″ × 1″). Cut 8 strips 1½″ × 20″ for half-square triangle Little Tiles.
■ FABRIC 2	1 fat quarter	Cut 10 strips 1″ × 20″; then cut into 184 plain Little Tiles (1″ × 1″). Cut 4 strips 1½″ × 20″ for half-square triangle Little Tiles.
■ FABRIC 3	2 fat quarters	Cut 16 strips 1″ × 20″; then cut into 304 plain Little Tiles (1″ × 1″). Cut 4 strips 1½″ × 20″ for half-square triangle Little Tiles.
■ FABRIC 4	2 fat quarters	Cut 12 strips 1″ × 20″; then cut into 232 plain Little Tiles (1″ × 1″). Cut 8 strips 1½″ × 20″ for half-square triangle Little Tiles.
▫ FABRIC 5	2 fat quarters	Cut 7 strips 1″ × 20″; then cut into 128 plain Little Tiles (1″ × 1″). Cut 8 strips 1½″ × 20″ for half-square triangle Little Tiles.
■ FABRIC 6: Full 40″ width for binding, sashing, and ends of cover fabric	⅝ yard	Cut 2 strips 1½″ × width of fabric for sashing between panels. Cut 2 strips 2½″ × width of fabric for binding. Cut 2 strips 5″ × width of fabric for drawstring section of cushion cover.

you will also need:

- Little Tile freezer-paper templates (see Cutting Freezer-Paper Tile Templates, page 6): 384 templates 1″ × 1″ (cut as needed)

- Lightweight fusible interfacing: 1½ yards cut into 1 piece 19″ × 51″ for center Darting Birds panel and 2 pieces 8″ × 51″ for the Trip Around the World panels

- Flannel or thin batting: 20″ × 26″

- Backing fabric, such as muslin: 20″ × 26″

- Drawstring cording: 2 yards

- Neck roll cushion insert: 18″ (or use leftover pieces of batting, plastic bags, or bubble wrap!)

MAKE THE NECK ROLL CUSHION

Seam allowances are ¼″ unless otherwise noted.

1. Make the plain Little Tiles (page 6) for the Darting Birds center panel and the 2 Trip Around the World side panels.

Make the half-square triangle Little Tiles (page 6). Use fabric scrimping (page 13).

Use the 1½″ × 20″ strips and piece 4 sets each of Fabrics 1 and 5, Fabrics 4 and 5, Fabrics 2 and 4, and Fabrics 1 and 3.

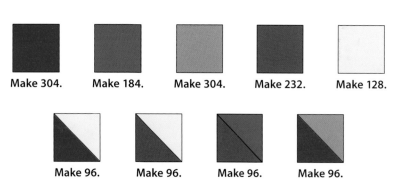

Make 304. Make 184. Make 304. Make 232. Make 128.

Make 96. Make 96. Make 96. Make 96.

Darting Birds Neck Roll Cushion Little Tiles

2. Make the Mini-Mosaic panels. Refer to the panel and sashing layout (page 70).

Make a Darting Birds panel and 2 Trip Around the World panels.

DARTING BIRDS NECK ROLL CUSHION is continued on page 70.

showtime
BADGE BAG

FINISHED SIZE: approximately 6″ wide × 8½″ high × 1½″ deep

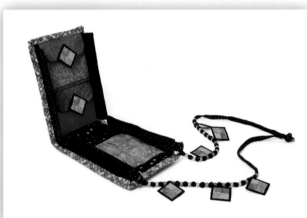

materials and cutting

Refer to Cutting Fabric Strips (page 5).

COLOR AND USE	YARDAGE	CUTTING
■ FABRIC 1	1 fat eighth	Cut 1 strip 1″ × 20″; then cut into 16 plain Little Tiles (1″ × 1″). Cut 2 strips 1″ × 20″; then cut into 4 pieces 1″ × 10″ for half-square triangle Little Tiles.
FABRIC 2	scrap 6″ × 6″	Cut 1 plain Little Tile (1″ × 1″) for center of Bear's Paw. Cut 16 plain Little Tiles (1″ × 1″) for pin tags and fasteners.
FABRIC 3	scrap 6″ × 6″	Cut 1 plain Little Tile (1″ × 1″) for Bear's Paw. Cut 16 plain Little Tiles (1″ × 1″) for pin tags and fasteners.
FABRIC 4	1 fat eighth	Cut 3 plain Little Tiles (1″ × 1″) for Bear's Paw. Cut 1 piece 6½″ × 8″ for glasses and cell phone pocket.
FABRIC 5	1 fat eighth	Cut 1 strip 1″ × 20″; then cut in half to 1″ × 10″ for half-square triangle Little Tiles for Bear's Paw. Cut 1 piece 5″ × 6½″ for lower interior pocket (tissue holder).
FABRIC 6	scrap 2″ × 2″	Cut 1 plain Little Tile (1″ × 1″) for Bear's Paw.
FABRIC 7	1 fat eighth	Cut 3 plain Little Tiles (1″ × 1″) for Bear's Paw. Cut 1 piece 7″ × 8″ for upper interior pocket.
FABRIC 8	1 fat eighth	Cut 1 strip 1″ × 20″; then cut in half to 1″ × 10″ for half-square triangle Little Tiles for Bear's Paw.
FABRIC 9	scrap 6″ × 6″	Cut 16 plain Little Tiles (1″ × 1″) for pin tags and fasteners. Cut 1 plain Little Tile (1″ × 1″) for Bear's Paw.
FABRIC 10	1 fat eighth	Cut 3 plain Little Tiles (1″ × 1″) for Bear's Paw. Cut 4 pieces 2½″ × 5″ for interior pocket flaps.
FABRIC 11	1 fat eighth	Cut 1 strip 1″ × 20″; then cut in half to 1″ × 10″ for half-square triangle Little Tiles for Bear's Paw.
FABRIC 12	scrap 6″ × 6″	Cut 16 plain Little Tiles (1″ × 1″) for pin tags and fasteners. Cut 1 plain Little Tile (1″ × 1″) for Bear's Paw.
FABRIC 13	1 scrap 4″ × 4″	Cut 3 plain Little Tiles (1″ × 1″) for Bear's Paw.
FABRIC 14	1 fat eighth	Cut 1 strip 1″ × 20″; then cut in half to 1″ × 10″ for half-square triangle Little Tiles for Bear's Paw.
FABRIC 15: 40″ width of fabric for body	¾ yard	Cut 1 strip 6″ × width of fabric; then cut into 2 pieces 6″ × 18½″ for exterior and interior of bag. Cut 1 piece 6″ × 10″ for exterior business card pocket. Cut 4 pieces 3½″ × 8½″ for bag sides.
FABRIC 16: Binding	1 fat quarter	Cut 1 square 15″ × 15″ for bias binding.

you will also need:

- Little Tile freezer-paper templates (see Cutting Freezer-Paper Tile Templates, page 6): 16 templates 1″ × 1″

- Lightweight fusible interfacing: 1 piece 8″ × 8″

- Paper-backed fusible web (Wonder Under or Steam-A-Seam): 1 piece 3½″ × 3½″ and 1 piece 4¾″ × 5½″

- fast2fuse: 2 pieces 5½″ × 18″ for bag exterior and interior, 4 pieces 1½″ × 8″ for bag sides, 1 piece 3½″ × 4½″ for inside purse pocket, 1 piece 3″ × 4½″ for tissue holder, 2 pieces 2″ × 4½″ for fastening flaps, and 8 pieces 1½″ × 1½″ for pin tags

- Quilter's Vinyl (by C&T Publishing): 1 piece 6″ × 11″

- D-rings: 2 pieces 1″

- Chain or long, slim bag strap: 1 yard

- Black grosgrain ribbon, 1″ wide: 2 pieces cut 2″ long

- Black hook and loop tape, ¾″ wide: 2 pieces 7¾″ long and 2 pieces ¾″ long

- Black elastic, ¼″ wide: ½ yard for interior pockets and loops

- Template plastic: 2″ × 4½″

- Invisible thread

- 6 small jump rings

MAKE THE BAG

Seam allowances are ¼″ unless otherwise noted.

1. Make the plain Little Tiles (page 6).

Make the half-square triangle Little Tiles (page 6).

Stitch the 1″ × 10″ strips together lengthwise into sets. Make 1 set each of Fabrics 1 and 5, Fabrics 1 and 8, Fabrics 1 and 11, and Fabrics 1 and 14. Cut out 4 half-square triangle Little Tiles from each set.

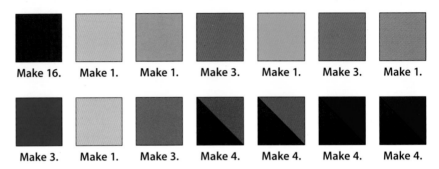

Make 16. Make 1. Make 1. Make 3. Make 1. Make 3. Make 1.

Make 3. Make 1. Make 3. Make 4. Make 4. Make 4. Make 4.

Showtime Badge Bag tiles

2. Make the Bear's Paw block for the Showtime Badge Bag front.

Bear's Paw block placement diagram

Block measures 4″ × 4″ from raw edge to raw edge (3½″ × 3½″ finished size).

SHOWTIME BADGE BAG is continued on page 70.

ohio ribbon star
CUSHION COVER

FINISHED SIZE: approximately 18″ × 18″

materials and cutting

Refer to Cutting Fabric Strips (page 5).

COLOR AND USE	YARDAGE	CUTTING
FABRIC 1: Centers and points of stars	1 fat quarter	Cut 1 strip 1½″ × 20″; then cut into 13 plain Big Tiles (1½″ × 1½″). Cut 8 strips 1½″ × 20″ for quarter-square triangle Big Tiles.
FABRIC 2: Background, backing, borders, and binding. (Note that I used 2 different blue fabrics that read similarly.)	2 fat quarters for background ¾ yard full 40″ width for backing, borders, and binding	**From the fat quarters:** Cut 4 strips 1½″ × 20″; then cut into 52 plain Big Tiles (1½″ × 1½″). Cut 8 strips 1½″ × 20″ for quarter-square triangle Big Tiles. Cut 4 strips 2″ × 20″ for half-square triangle Big Tiles. **From the full-width yardage:** Cut 2 strips 2″ × width of fabric for border. Cut 2 strips 2½″ × width of fabric for binding. Cut 2 pieces 13″ × 20″ for back of cushion.
FABRIC 3: Ribbons	1 fat quarter	Cut 2 strips 1½″ × 20″; then cut into 24 plain Big Tiles (1½″ × 1½″). Cut 2 strips 1½″ × 20″ for quarter-square triangle Big Tiles. Cut 2 strips 2″ × 20″ for half-square triangle Big Tiles.
FABRIC 4: Ribbons	1 fat quarter	Cut 2 strips 1½″ × 20″; then cut into 24 plain Big Tiles (1½″ × 1½″). Cut 2 strips 1½″ × 20″ for quarter-square triangle Big Tiles. Cut 2 strips 2″ × 20″ for half-square triangle Big Tiles.

you will also need:

- Big Tile freezer-paper templates (see Cutting Freezer-Paper Tile Templates, page 6): 112 templates 1½″ × 1½″

- Muslin or similar fabric: ⅔ yard for lining, cut into 1 piece 20″ × 20″ and 2 pieces 10″ × 20″

- Flannel or thin batting: 1 piece 20″ × 20″ and 2 pieces 11″ × 20″

- Lightweight fusible interfacing: 24″ × 24″ piece

- Large button for cushion cover closure: 1 piece ⅞″ diameter

- Square cushion insert: 1 piece 18″ × 18″

MAKE THE CUSHION COVER

Seam allowances are ¼″ unless otherwise noted.

1. Make the plain Big Tiles (page 7).

Make the half-square triangle Big Tiles (page 8). Use the 2″-wide strips to piece 2 sets each of Fabrics 2 and 3, and Fabrics 2 and 4, using fabric scrimping (page 13).

Make the quarter-square triangle Big Tiles (page 8). Use the 1½″-wide strips to piece 8 sets of Fabrics 1 and 2, and 2 sets of Fabrics 3 and 4.

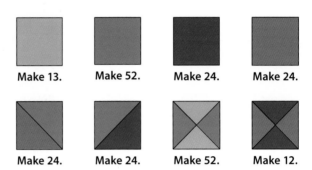

Make 13. Make 52. Make 24. Make 24.

Make 24. Make 24. Make 52. Make 12.

Ohio Ribbon Star tiles

2. Make the Ohio Ribbon Star Mini-Mosaic panel. The panel measures 15½″ × 15½″ from raw edge to raw edge (15″ × 15″ finished size).

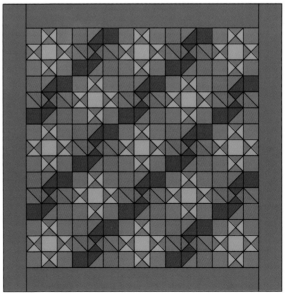

Ohio Ribbon Star Cushion Cover front diagram

OHIO RIBBON STAR CUSHION COVER is continued on page 74.

playing bridge
CUSHION COVER

FINISHED SIZE: approximately 18″ × 18″

materials and cutting

Refer to Cutting Fabric Strips (page 5).

COLOR AND USE	YARDAGE	CUTTING
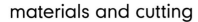 **FABRIC 1:** Squares	3 fat quarters	Cut 18 strips 1½″ × 20″; then cut 2 of these strips into 24 plain Big Tiles (1½″ × 1½″). Cut 8 strips 1¾″ × 20″.
FABRIC 2: Squares and inner border	1 fat quarter	Cut 4 strips 1½″ × 20″. Cut 2 strips 1″ × 20″.
FABRIC 3: Squares and inner border	1 fat quarter	Cut 4 strips 1½″ × 20″. Cut 2 strips 1″ × 20″.
FABRIC 4: Squares and inner border	1 fat quarter	Cut 4 strips 1½″ × 20″. Cut 2 strips 1″ × 20″.
FABRIC 5: Squares and inner border	1 fat quarter	Cut 4 strips 1½″ × 20″. Cut 2 strips 1″ × 20″.
FABRIC 6: Squares	1 fat quarter	Cut 6 strips 1½″ × 20″. Cut 2 strips 1″ × 20″.
FABRIC 7: Squares	1 fat quarter	Cut 6 strips 1½″ × 20″. Cut 2 strips 1″ × 20″.
FABRIC 8: Squares, backing, and binding	1 fat quarter for squares ⅔ yard full-width 40″ fabric for backing and binding	**From fat quarter:** Cut 6 strips 1½″ × 20″. Cut 2 strips 1″ × 20″. **From full 40″-width yardage:** Cut 2 strips 2½″ × width of fabric for binding and 2 pieces 13″ × 20″ for back.
FABRIC 9: Squares	1 fat quarter	Cut 6 strips 1½″ × 20″. Cut 2 strips 1″ × 20″.

you will also need:

- Big Tile freezer-paper templates (see Cutting Freezer-Paper Tile Templates, page 6): 192 templates 1½″ × 1½″ (cut as needed)

- Muslin or similar fabric: ⅔ yard for lining, cut into 1 piece 20″ × 20″ and 2 pieces 10″ × 20″

- Flannel or thin batting: 1 piece 20″ × 20″ and 2 pieces 11″ × 20″

- Lightweight fusible interfacing: 24″ × 24″

- Large button for cushion cover closure, ⅞″ diameter

- Square cushion insert 18″ × 18″

MAKE THE CUSHION COVER

Seam allowances are ¼″ unless otherwise noted.

1. Make the plain Big Tiles (page 7).

Make the half-square triangle Big Tiles (page 8). Use 1½″-wide strips sewn into 2 sets each of Fabrics 1 and 6, Fabrics 1 and 7, Fabrics 1 and 8, and Fabrics 1 and 9. Cut 16 half-square triangle Big Tiles from each of the 4 color combinations.

Make the half- and quarter-square triangle Big Tiles (page 9). Use 1½″-wide strips sewn into 2 sets each of Fabrics 1 and 6, Fabrics 1 and 7, Fabrics 1 and 8, and Fabrics 1 and 9. Cut the sets into 16 segments 1½″ wide in each of the 4 color combinations. Sew these segments onto the 1½″-wide strips of Fabrics 5, 2, 4, and 3.

Make the quarter-square triangle Big Tiles (page 8). Use 1½″-wide strips sewn into 2 sets each of Fabrics 2 and 3, and Fabrics 4 and 5. Cut the sets into 16 segments 1½″ wide in each of the 2 color combinations; then make the tiles from the segments.

Make the corner triangle Big Tiles (page 10). Use 1¾″-wide strips of Fabric 1 and 1″-wide strips of Fabrics 6, 7, 8, and 9, sewn into 2 sets each of Fabrics 1 and 6, Fabrics 1 and 7, Fabrics 1 and 8, and Fabrics 1 and 9.

Make the four-patch Big Tiles (page 11). Use the 1″-wide strips of Fabrics 2, 3, 4, and 5 sewn into 1 set each of Fabrics 2 and 3, and Fabrics 4 and 5.

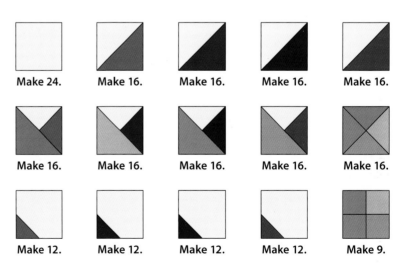

Make 24.   Make 16.   Make 16.   Make 16.   Make 16.

Make 16.   Make 16.   Make 16.   Make 16.   Make 16.

Make 12.   Make 12.   Make 12.   Make 12.   Make 9.

Playing Bridge tiles

2. Make the Playing Bridge Mini-Mosaic block.

The block measures 15½″ × 15½″ from raw edge to raw edge (15″ × 15″ finished size).

Playing Bridge block placement diagram

3. Add the borders.

First border (½″ finished size) Refer to Playing Bridge Cushion Cover front with second border added (at right). Cut the remaining 1″-wide strips of Fabrics 2, 3, 4, and 5 to measure 1″ × 16″, and stitch them to the Playing Bridge block. Use a partial seam to stitch on the first border for ease in piecing. (Stitch three-quarters of the first border on, leaving the end free. Moving counterclockwise, stitch the second border on completely. Continue around. Stitch the end of the first border after the last border has been stitched in place.) The block measures 16½″ × 16½″ from raw edge to raw edge.

Second border (1″ finished width) Make a strip set of 8 strips by stitching the 2 remaining 1½″ strips of Fabrics 6, 7, 8, and 9 to each other lengthwise using a ¼″ seam allowance. Press. The set measures 8½″ × 20″. Rotary cut 9 segments 1½″ wide from the set, and join the segments end to end in 1 long strip set.

Cut 1½″-wide segments.

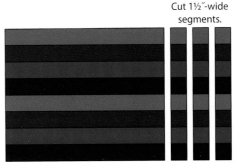

Second border construction

From this set unpick the seam allowances to make 2 pieces that are 16 segments in length for the side borders, and stitch them onto the block. Press. Unpick 2 pieces that are 18 segments in length for the top and bottom borders and stitch them onto the quilt. Press. The block now measures 18½″ × 18½″.

**Playing Bridge Cushion Cover front
with second border added**

4. Sandwich and baste the block using the 20″ × 20″ piece of very thin batting or flannel and the 20″ × 20″ piece of muslin. Quilt as desired.

5. Make the block into a cushion cover.

TO COMPLETE THE CUSHION COVER
Follow the instructions for the Ohio Ribbon Star Cushion Cover (page 37).

lipari pinwheel
LAPTOP BAG

FINISHED SIZE: approximately
18″ wide × 15″ high × 4″ deep

materials and cutting

Refer to Cutting Fabric Strips (page 5).

COLOR AND USE	YARDAGE	CUTTING
FABRIC 1: Squares, borders, bag straps	2½ yards full width 40″	Cut 15 strips 3″ × width of fabric; then cut into 30 strips 3″ × 20″ for corner triangle Big Tiles. **From the remaining fabric, lengthwise grain:** Cut 1 strip 2½″ × 44½″ for top border of bag. Cut 1 strip 4½″ × 44½″ for bottom border of bag. Cut 2 strips 2¾″ × 44½″ for bag handles and shoulder strap. Join end to end. Cut 2 strips 1¼″ × 44½″ for bag handles and shoulder strap. Join end to end. Cut 1 strip 4½″ × 44½″; then rotary cut this strip into the following: • 4 pieces 4½″ × 6″ each for the ends of the shoulder strap and D-ring loops • 4 pieces 4½″ × 3″ each for the ends of the bag handles
FABRICS 2–16	1 fat quarter each	Cut 2 strips 3″ × 20″ from each fabric for corner-square triangle Big Tiles. Cut 1 strip 1½″ × 20″ from each fabric for bag handles and strap. **From the remaining fabric:** Cut 10 pieces 6½″ × 18½″ (colors of your choice) for laptop protective cover bag insert.
FABRIC 17: Bag lining	1½ yards full width 40″	**From the lengthwise grain of full-width fabric:** Cut 1 piece 18½″ × 44½″ for bag lining. Cut 1 piece 12½″ × 44½″ for bag inner pockets. Cut 1 piece 1″ × 44½″ for laptop insert ties. Cut 1 piece 6½″ × 6½″ for fastening flap. Cut 1 piece 5″ × 36″ for foam core stabilizer cover.

you will also need:

- Big Tile freezer-paper templates (see Cutting Freezer-Paper Tile Templates, page 6), 1½″ × 1½″ and marked with corner triangle line: 132 (start with this number and cut more as needed)

- Lightweight fusible interfacing, 36″ wide: 2¼ yards cut to measure 72″ × 20″

- Fusible fleece or Fusible Volume Fleece (by Vilene), 36″ wide: 2½ yards

- Heavyweight fusible interfacing for bag handles and shoulder strap: 4 pieces 1½″ × 25″ and 2 pieces 1½″ × 37″, plus 2 pieces 4½″ × 6″ for D-ring loops

- Stiff plastic canvas: 1 piece 3½″ × 17½″

- Foam core: 1 piece ½″ thick (or 2 pieces ¼″ thick), cut 3½″ × 17½″ for stabilizer insert

- Protective bag feet (the type with "wings" that open flat like paper fasteners): 4 large pieces

- D-rings: 2 pieces, 1½″ for removable bag shoulder strap

- Trigger hooks, gate ring hooks, or swivel hooks for shoulder strap: 2 pieces, 1½″

- Sew-in hook and loop tape, ¾″ wide: 1 small piece approximately 2″ long

- Batting remnant: Approximately 8″ × 19″ for covering foam core stabilizer insert

- Template plastic: 1 piece cut 2″ × 2″

Cut the Fusible Fleece

Seam allowances are ¼″ unless otherwise noted.

1. Cut the fusible fleece or Fusible Volume Fleece into the following pieces:

2 pieces 18″ × 44″ for bag exterior and bag lining

1 piece 18″ × 30″ for laptop protective cover bag insert

1 piece 6″ × 36″ for interior pocket section

1 piece 6″ × 8″ for interior pocket section

1 piece 3″ × 6″ for fastening flap on laptop pocket

2 pieces 1½″ × 23½″ for bag handles

1 piece 1½″ × 35½″ for shoulder strap

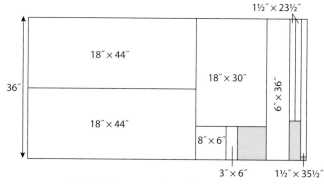

Fusible fleece cutting diagram

MAKE THE BAG

Seam allowances are ¼″ unless otherwise noted.

2. Make the double corner triangle Big Tiles (page 10).

Use the 3″ × 20″ strips of Fabrics 2 through 16. Sew each strip into a set with a 3″ × 20″ strip of Fabric 1. Use fabric scrimping (page 13). Each set yields 12 black tiles with colored corner triangles (yang) and 12 colored tiles with black corner triangles (yin). You end up with 720 tiles in total and 528 tiles are used for the bag. You can play with various color layouts, and see the Tip for a leftover tiles project (page 78) that uses some of the remaining tiles.

Yin tiles cut from strip set, and yang tiles from another strip set

3. Make the Lipari Pinwheel Mini-Mosaic panel.

Use 528 of the corner triangle Big Tiles (264 yin tiles and 264 yang tiles). The panel measures 12½″ × 44½″.

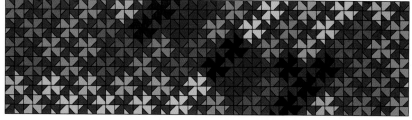

Lipari Pinwheel block placement diagram

LIPARI PINWHEEL LAPTOP BAG is continued on page 75.

tenley's teatime tango
BOOK COVER

FINISHED SIZE: 6″ wide × 9″ high × ¾″ deep

materials and cutting

Refer to Making Tile Blanks for Individual Tiles (page 15).

COLOR AND USE	YARDAGE	CUTTING
FABRIC 1	1 fat eighth	Cut 12 pieces 1½″ × 1½″. Cut 8 pieces 1½″ × 2½″.
FABRIC 2	6″ × 6″	Cut 2 pieces 1½″ × 1½″. Cut 3 pieces 1½″ × 2½″.
FABRIC 3	2″ × 2″	Cut 1 piece 1½″ × 1½″.
FABRIC 4	6″ × 6″	Cut 2 pieces 1½″ × 1½″. Cut 3 pieces 1½″ × 2½″.
FABRIC 5	2″ × 2″	Cut 1 piece 1½″ × 1½″.
FABRIC 6	6″ × 6″	Cut 2 pieces 1½″ × 1½″. Cut 3 pieces 1½″ × 2½″.
FABRIC 7	2″ × 2″	Cut 1 piece 1½″ × 1½″.
FABRIC 8	6″ × 6″	Cut 2 pieces 1½″ × 1½″. Cut 3 pieces 1½″ × 2½″.
FABRIC 9	2″ × 2″	Cut 1 piece 1½″ × 1½″.
FABRIC 10:* Outer book cover and pockets	1 fat quarter print for book cover (depends on book size)	Cut 1 piece 9½″ × 13¼″. Cut 2 pieces 6½″ × 9½″ for pockets.
FABRIC 11:* Lining	1 fat quarter print for lining book cover (depends on book size)	Cut 1 piece 9½″ × 13¼″.

* The book covered here measures 5¾″ wide × 8½″ high × ¾″ deep. You may need more or less of Fabrics 10 and 11 depending on the size of the book you wish to cover.

you will also need:

- Freezer paper for templates: 13 squares 1½″ × 1½″

- Lightweight fusible interfacing: 1 piece 8″ × 8″

- Paper-backed fusible web: 1 piece cut 5″ × 5″ and marked with a centered 4″ × 4″ square

- Fabric glue. I prefer Roxanne Glue-Baste-It.

- Invisible thread

- Batting: 1 piece 9½″ × 13¼″ and 2 pieces 3″ × 9″ (depends on book size)

- Muslin: 1 piece 9½″ × 13¼″ (depends on book size)

- Ribbon for page marker, ½″ wide: 1 piece 10″ long (not shown in sample)

- Notebook: 1, measuring 5¾″ wide × 8½″ high × ¾″ deep

TIP

Make a custom-measured book cover by first placing the book on a large piece of plain paper.

A. Trace around the closed book (5¾″ × 8½″ in sample).

B. Trace around the spine of the book (¾″ × 8½″).

C. Trace around the closed book again (5¾″ × 8½″).

D. Add ½″ all around the outer edge.

Use the resulting measurements to cut the Fabric 10 and Fabric 11 lining pieces (9½″ × 13¼″).

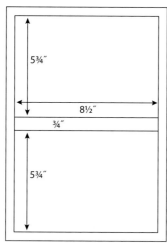

How to make custom-fitted book cover

MAKE THE BOOK COVER

Seam allowances are ¼″ unless otherwise noted.

1. Make the plain Big Tiles (page 7).

Cut 8 tiles of Fabric 1, and a tile each of Fabrics 3, 5, 7, and 9.

Make the half-square triangle Big Tiles (page 8).

Use the 1½″ × 2½″ strips sewn into 2 sets each of Fabrics 1 and 2, Fabrics 1 and 4, Fabrics 1 and 6, and Fabrics 1 and 8.

Make the half- and quarter-square triangle Big Tiles (page 9).

Use the 1½″ × 1½″ squares sewn into 1 set each of Fabrics 1 and 8, Fabrics 1 and 2, Fabrics 1 and 4, and Fabrics 1 and 6. Use the remaining 1½″ × 2½″ strips to stitch and cut a tile each of Fabrics 1, 2, and 8; Fabrics 1, 4, and 2; Fabrics 1, 6, and 4; and Fabrics 1, 8, and 6 (colors listed clockwise starting at the top of the tile).

Make the quarter-square triangle Big Tiles (page 8).

Use the remaining 1½″ × 1½″ squares to stitch and cut a tile of Fabrics 2, 4, 6, and 8.

Make 8. Make 1. Make 1. Make 1. Make 1.

Make 2. Make 2. Make 2. Make 2. Make 1.

Make 1. Make 1. Make 1. Make 1.

Tenley's Teatime Tango block Big Tiles

2. Make the Tenley's Teatime Tango Mini-Mosaic block. The block measures 5½″ × 5½″ from raw edge to raw edge (5″ × 5″ finished size).

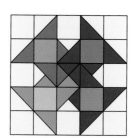

Tenley's Teatime Tango block placement diagram

TENLEY'S TEATIME TANGO BOOK COVER is continued on page 78.

wedding rose
TABLE RUNNER

FINISHED SIZE: 21″ × 61″

materials and cutting

Refer to Cutting Fabric Strips (page 5).

COLOR AND USE	YARDAGE	CUTTING
FABRIC 1:* Alternate blocks, Big Tile squares, and first border	3 fat quarters ¾ yard, 40″ width, for first border and alternate blocks	Cut 6 strips 1½″ × 20″; then cut into 68 plain Big Tiles (1½″ × 1½″). Cut 10 strips 2″ × 20″ for half-square triangle Big Tiles. Cut 12 strips 1½″ × 20″ for stem-and-triangle Big Tiles. **From 40″-width fabric:** Cut 3 strips 5½″ × width of fabric; then cut these into 16 squares 5½″ × 5½″. Cut 4 strips 1½″ × width of fabric for first border; then cut 1 strip into 2 pieces 1½″ × 17½″; stitch the remaining 3 strips together end to end and cut into 2 pieces 1½″ × 55½″
FABRIC 2	1 fat eighth	Cut 2 strips 1½″ × 20″; then cut into 17 plain Big Tiles (1½″ × 1½″).
FABRIC 3: Binding	2 fat quarters ½ yard, 40″ width	Cut 10 strips 2″ × 20″ for half-square triangle Big Tiles. Cut 6 strips ¾″ × 20″ for stem-and-triangle Big Tiles. From 40″-width fabric, cut 5 strips 2½″ × width of fabric for binding.
FABRIC 4: Second border	2 fat quarters	Cut 6 strips 1½″ × 20″; then cut into 68 plain Big Tiles (1½″ × 1½″). Cut 5 strips 2″ × 20″ for half-square triangle Big Tiles. Cut 8 strips 1″ × 20″ for second border; then cut 2 strips into 2 pieces 1″ × 18½″ and stitch 6 strips together end to end and cut into 2 pieces 1″ × 57½″.
FABRIC 5	1 fat quarter	Cut 6 strips 2″ × 20″ for stem-and-triangle Big Tiles.
FABRIC 6: Third border	⅜ yard, 40″ width	Cut 5 strips 2″ × width of fabric; then cut 2 strips into 2 pieces 2″ × 21½″ and stitch 3 strips together end to end and cut into 2 pieces 2″ × 58½″.
FABRIC 7	1 fat quarter	Cut 5 strips 2″ × 20″ for half-square triangle Big Tiles.

* For Fabric 1, I used a fabric with gradated colors to achieve the variation.

you will also need:

- Big Tile freezer-paper templates (see Cutting Freezer-Paper Tile Templates, page 6): 272 templates 1½″ × 1½″ (cut as needed)
- Backing fabric, full 40″ width: 1⅓ yards
- Batting: 64″ × 25″
- Lightweight fusible interfacing: 2 yards, cut into 17 squares 8″ × 8″

MAKE THE TABLE RUNNER

Seam allowances are ¼″ unless otherwise noted.

1. Make the plain Big Tiles (page 7).

Make the half-square triangle Big Tiles (page 8). Make the tiles using the 2″-wide strips, combining Fabrics 1 and 3, and Fabrics 4 and 7. Apply fabric scrimping (page 13).

Make the stem-and-triangle Big Tiles (page 12). Make 6 sets each using 2 strips 1½″ wide of Fabric 1, with a ¾″ strip of Fabric 3 between them, for the 1½″-wide stem segments. Additionally, use a 2″-wide strip of Fabric 5 to complete the squares.

Make 68.   Make 17.   Make 68.

Make 136.   Make 68.   Make 68.

Wedding Rose Big Tiles

2. Make the 17 Wedding Rose blocks.

Blocks measure 5½″ × 5½″ from raw edge to raw edge (5″ × 5″ finished size).

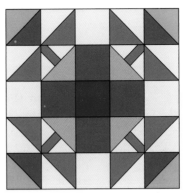

Wedding Rose block placement diagram

3. Make the Wedding Rose Table Runner.

Stitch the Wedding Rose blocks to the 5½″ × 5½″ squares of Fabric 1 in rows, pressing the seams in opposite directions in alternating rows. Join the rows. Press. Next, add the Fabric 1, 4, and 6 borders.

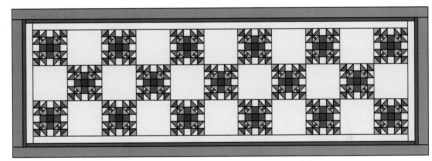

Wedding Rose Table Runner assembly

4. Cut 2 pieces 25″ × width of fabric from the backing fabric. Trim the pieces to 32¼″ long. Stitch the short ends together to make a backing piece 25″ × 64″.

5. Referring to Quilting Mini-Mosaics (page 18), sandwich, baste, and quilt as desired. Referring to Binding (page 18), join and bind with 2½″-wide strips of Fabric 3.

threesallations
WALL QUILT

FINISHED SIZE: 16″ × 44″

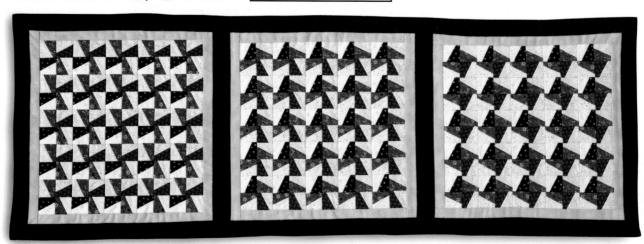

materials and cutting

Refer to Cutting Fabric Strips (page 5).

COLOR AND USE	YARDAGE	CUTTING
FABRIC 1	2 fat quarters	Cut 10 strips 2½″ × 20″. (Or if you don't want to use fabric scrimping, cut 20 strips 1½″ × 20″.)
FABRIC 2	2 fat quarters	Cut 10 strips 2½″ × 20″. (Or if you don't want to use fabric scrimping, cut 20 strips 1½″ × 20″.)
FABRIC 3	1 fat quarter	Cut 5 strips 2½″ × 20″. (Or if you don't want to use fabric scrimping, cut 10 strips 1½″ × 20″.)
FABRIC 4	1 fat quarter	Cut 5 strips 2½″ × 20″. (Or if you don't want to use fabric scrimping, cut 10 strips 1½″ × 20″.)
FABRIC 5	1 fat quarter	Cut 5 strips 2½″ × 20″. (Or if you don't want to use fabric scrimping, cut 10 strips 1½″ × 20″.)
FABRIC 6	1 fat quarter	Cut 5 strips 2½″ × 20″. (Or if you don't want to use fabric scrimping, cut 10 strips 1½″ × 20″.)
FABRIC 7: Block inner border	¼ yard full 40″-width fabric	Cut 4 strips 1½″ × width of fabric; and then cut them into 6 pieces 1½″ × 10½″ and 6 pieces 1½″ × 12½″.
FABRIC 8: Sashing, outer border, and binding	¾ yard full 40″-width fabric	Cut 9 strips 2½″ by width of fabric; from these strips, do the following: Cut 1 strip into 2 pieces 2½″ × 12½″ for sashing. Cut 2 strips into 2 pieces 2½″ × 40½″ (add a small amount of fabric to get to the correct length, if necessary). Cut 1 strip into 2 pieces 2½″ × 16½″. (The remaining 5 strips are for binding the wallhanging.)

you will also need:

- Freezer paper for templates (see Cutting Freezer-Paper Tile Templates, page 6):

  150 squares rotary cut 1½″ × 1½″ and marked to make half-square trapezoid Big Tiles (see template pattern, at right); *and*

  150 squares rotary cut 1½″ × 1½″ and marked to make half-square trapezoid *reverse* Big Tiles (see template pattern, at right).

- Lightweight fusible interfacing: 3 squares 17″ × 17″

- Backing fabric: 20″ × 48″

- Batting: 20″ × 48″

MAKE THE WALL QUILT

Seam allowances are ¼″ unless otherwise noted.

1. Make the half-square trapezoid Big Tiles and the half-square trapezoid reverse Big Tiles (page 11).

Note: These tiles are not identical—they are mirror images of each other.

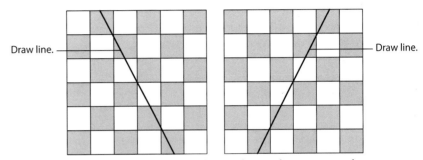

Half-square trapezoid Big Tile template and reverse template

Piece 5 sets each of Fabrics 1 and 4, Fabrics 1 and 5, Fabrics 2 and 3, and Fabrics 2 and 6. Both types of tiles (such as tiles A and AR, or *A reversed*) are made from the same fabric sets—it is the direction of the line on the freezer-paper template that makes the difference. Apply fabric scrimping (page 13) to make the tiles.

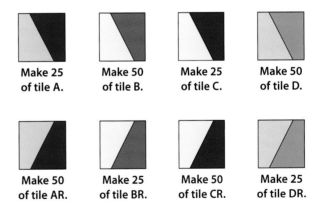

Make 25 of tile A.   **Make 50 of tile B.**   **Make 25 of tile C.**   **Make 50 of tile D.**

Make 50 of tile AR.   **Make 25 of tile BR.**   **Make 50 of tile CR.**   **Make 25 of tile DR.**

Half-square trapezoid Big Tiles for Threesallations Wall Quilt

2. Make the 3 Mini-Mosaic blocks.

■ Windmill block—25 tiles each of A, B, C, D

■ Flying Starlings block—25 tiles each of AR, B, CR, D

■ Hound's-Tooth block—25 tiles each of AR, BR, CR, DR

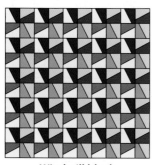

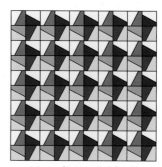

Windmill block   Flying Starlings block   Hound's-Tooth block

Tile and 3 tessellating block placement diagrams

Each block measures 10½″ × 10½″ from raw edge to raw edge (10″ × 10″ finished).

3. Add the Fabric 7 inner border to the blocks, stitching the sides first and pressing. Add the top and bottom borders and press.

4. Add the sashing and then the Fabric 8 outer borders to the bordered blocks.

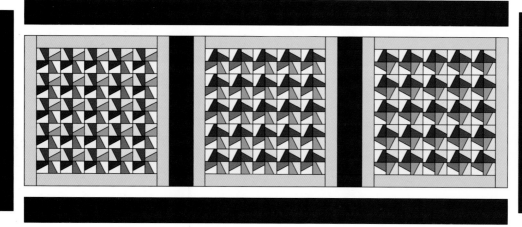

Add inner border, sashing, and outer border to make quilt top.

5. Referring to Quilting Mini-Mosaics (page 18), sandwich, baste, and quilt as desired. Bind with the remaining 2½″-wide strips of Fabric 8. Join the binding strips and bind using your favorite method; see Binding (page 18).

tesserae
SAMPLER QUILT

QUILT SIZE: 42″ × 50″

BLOCK SIZE: 6″ × 6″ (finished)

BLOCK SETTING: 5 blocks × 6 blocks

SASHING AND SASHING BORDER: 2″

materials and cutting

Following the chart, cut the fabric for all the blocks into 1½˝ × 20˝ strips; then subcut into 1½˝ × 1½˝ squares and 1½˝ × 2½˝ rectangles to make the blanks for the tiles needed for the blocks (see Making Tile Blanks for Individual Tiles, page 15). Make a block at a time; then cut more blanks as needed.

COLOR AND USE	YARDAGE	CUTTING
FABRIC 1: Cream/yellow	7 fat quarters	Cut 72 strips 1½˝ × 20˝; subcut 21 strips into 1½˝ × 1½˝ squares and 51 strips into 1½˝ × 2½˝ rectangles.
FABRIC 2: Dark red	2 fat quarters	Cut 16 strips 1½˝ × 20˝; subcut 6 strips into 1½˝ × 1½˝ squares and 10 strips into 1½˝ × 2½˝ rectangles.
FABRIC 3: Dark blue	3 fat quarters	Cut 32 strips 1½˝ × 20˝; subcut 7 strips into 1½˝ × 1½˝ squares and 25 strips into 1½˝ × 2½˝ rectangles.
FABRIC 4: Dark gold	2 fat quarters	Cut 16 strips 1½˝ × 20˝; subcut 6 strips into 1½˝ × 1½˝ squares and 10 strips into 1½˝ × 2½˝ rectangles.
FABRIC 5: Medium/dark green	2 fat quarters	Cut 19 strips 1½˝ × 20˝; subcut 6 strips into 1½˝ × 1½˝ squares and 13 strips into 1½˝ × 2½˝ rectangles.
FABRIC 6: Red	2 fat quarters	Cut 18 strips 1½˝ × 20˝; subcut 6 strips into 1½˝ × 1½˝ squares and 12 strips into 1½˝ × 2½˝ rectangles.
FABRIC 7: Medium/light blue	2 fat quarters	Cut 17 strips 1½˝ × 20˝; subcut 6 strips into 1½˝ × 1½˝ squares and 11 strips into 1½˝ × 2½˝ rectangles.
FABRIC 8: Medium gold	2 fat quarters	Cut 19 strips 1½˝ × 20˝; subcut 7 strips into 1½˝ × 1½˝ squares and 12 strips into 1½˝ × 2½˝ rectangles.
FABRIC 9: Medium green	2 fat quarters	Cut 20 strips 1½˝ × 20˝; subcut 5 strips into 1½˝ × 1½˝ squares and 15 strips into 1½˝ × 2½˝ rectangles.

you will also need:

- Big Tile freezer-paper templates (see Cutting Freezer-Paper Tile Templates, page 6): start with 120 templates 1½˝ × 1½˝ (cut more as needed)

- 2 full-width 40˝ fabrics for sashing: tan ¾ yard and darkest green ¾ yard. Rotary cut 16 strips of each fabric 1½˝ × width of fabric.

- Full-width 40˝ fabric for binding: ½ yard. Rotary cut 6 strips 2½˝ × width of fabric.

- Backing fabric: 2⅝ yards

- Lightweight fusible interfacing: 30 squares 10˝ × 10˝

- Batting: crib size 45˝ × 60˝

MAKE THE QUILT

Seam allowances are ¼˝ unless otherwise noted.

1. Make each tile type by referring to the indicated pages.

Plain Big Tiles (page 7)

Half-square rectangle Big Tiles (page 7)

Half-square triangle Big Tiles (page 8)

Quarter-square triangle Big Tiles (page 8)

Half- and quarter-square triangle Big Tiles (page 9)

Corner triangle Big Tiles (page 10)

Stem Big Tiles (page 23)

Referring to the quilt layout diagram (page 63), the block layout configuration is as follows: Rows are labeled A–F from top to bottom and columns are listed as 1–5 from left to right. For example, location B4 refers to row B, column 4.

Quilt instruction steps continue on page 63.

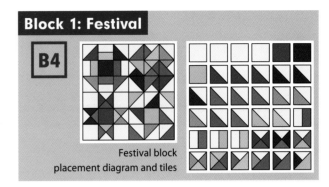

Block 1: Festival

B4

Festival block placement diagram and tiles

Plain Big Tiles (7)

4 tiles of Fabric 1

1 tile each of Fabric 2, Fabric 3, and Fabric 8

Half-square triangle Big Tiles (16)

3 tiles each of Fabrics 1 and 2, Fabrics 1 and 3, Fabrics 1 and 4, and Fabrics 1 and 5

1 tile each of Fabrics 1 and 6, Fabrics 1 and 7, Fabrics 1 and 8, and Fabrics 1 and 9

Half-square rectangle Big Tiles (4)

1 tile each of Fabrics 1 and 6, Fabrics 1 and 7, Fabrics 1 and 8, and Fabrics 1 and 9

Quarter-square triangle Big Tiles (colors clockwise starting at top of tile) (5)

1 tile each of Fabrics 1, 2 ,6, and 2; Fabrics 1, 3, 7, and 3; Fabrics 1, 4, 8, and 4; Fabrics 1, 5, 9, and 5; and Fabrics 9, 6, 7, and 8

Half- and quarter-square triangle Big Tiles (colors clockwise starting at top of tile: quarter, half, quarter) (4)

1 tile each of Fabrics 1, 9, and 4; Fabrics 1, 6, and 5; Fabrics 1, 7, and 2; and Fabrics 1, 8, and 3

Block 2: Milky Way

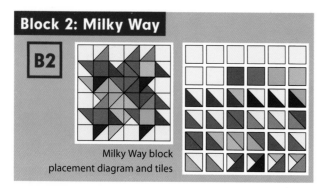

B2

Milky Way block
placement diagram and tiles

Plain Big Tiles (12)

8 tiles of Fabric 1

1 tile each of Fabric 6, Fabric 7, Fabric 8, and Fabric 9

Half-square triangle Big Tiles (20)

2 tiles each of Fabrics 1 and 2, Fabrics 1 and 3,
Fabrics 1 and 4, and Fabrics 1 and 5

1 tile each of Fabrics 2 and 9, Fabrics 3 and 8, Fabrics 4 and 7,
Fabrics 5 and 6, Fabrics 6 and 7, Fabrics 6 and 9, Fabrics 8 and 9,
Fabrics 7 and 8, Fabrics 1 and 6, Fabrics 1 and 7, Fabrics 1 and 8,
and Fabrics 1 and 9

**Half- and quarter-square triangle Big Tiles (colors clock-
wise starting at top of tile: quarter, half, quarter) (4)**

1 tile each of Fabrics 7, 2, and 1; Fabrics 6, 3, and 1,
Fabrics 9, 4, and 1; and Fabrics 8, 5, and 1

Block 4: Wyoming Valley

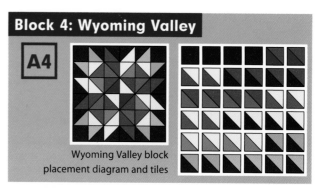

A4

Wyoming Valley block
placement diagram and tiles

Plain Big Tiles (4)

4 tiles of Fabric 3

Half-square triangle Big Tiles (32)

2 tiles each of Fabrics 2 and 6, and Fabrics 1 and 6

4 tiles each of Fabrics 3 and 6, Fabrics 6 and 7,
Fabrics 1 and 4, Fabrics 1 and 3, Fabrics 1 and 5,
Fabrics 3 and 8, and Fabrics 3 and 9

Block 3: Jewels

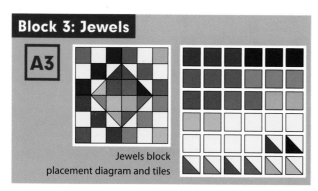

A3

Jewels block
placement diagram and tiles

Plain Big Tiles (28)

8 tiles of Fabric 1

3 tiles each of Fabric 2, Fabric 3, Fabric 4, and Fabric 5

2 tiles each of Fabric 6, Fabric 7, Fabric 8, and Fabric 9

Half-square triangle Big Tiles (8)

1 tile each of Fabrics 1 and 2, Fabrics 1 and 3,
Fabrics 1 and 4, Fabrics 1 and 5, Fabrics 1 and 6,
Fabrics 1 and 7, Fabrics 1 and 8, and Fabrics 1 and 9

Block 5: Flying Fan

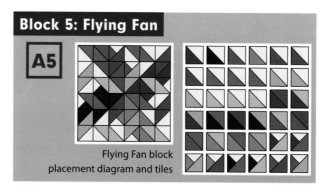

A5

Flying Fan block
placement diagram and tiles

Half-square triangle Big Tiles (28)

3 tiles each of Fabrics 1 and 6, Fabrics 1 and 7,
Fabrics 1 and 8, and Fabrics 1 and 9

1 tile each of Fabrics 1 and 2, Fabrics 1 and 3, Fabrics 1 and 4,
Fabrics 1 and 5, Fabrics 2 and 6, Fabrics 2 and 9, Fabrics 2 and 8,
Fabrics 3 and 7, Fabrics 3 and 6, Fabrics 3 and 8, Fabrics 4 and 9,
Fabrics 4 and 6, Fabrics 4 and 7, Fabrics 5 and 9, Fabrics 5 and 7,
and Fabrics 5 and 8

**Half- and quarter-square triangle Big Tiles (colors clock-
wise starting at top of tile: quarter, half, quarter) (8)**

1 tile each of Fabrics 1, 9, and 2; Fabrics 1, 7, and 2;
Fabrics 1, 8, and 5; Fabrics 1, 6, and 5; Fabrics 1, 7, and 3;
Fabrics 1, 9, and 3; Fabrics 1, 6, and 4; and Fabrics 1, 8, and 4

Block 6: Square Dance

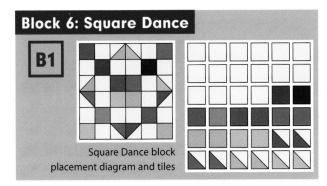

Square Dance block placement diagram and tiles

Plain Big Tiles (28)

16 tiles of Fabric 1

2 tiles each of Fabric 6, Fabric 7, Fabric 8, and Fabric 9

1 tile each of Fabric 2, Fabric 3, Fabric 4, and Fabric 5

Half-square triangle Big Tiles (8)

2 tiles each of Fabrics 1 and 6, Fabrics 1 and 7, Fabrics 1 and 8, and Fabrics 1 and 9

Block 8: Ring of Rosies

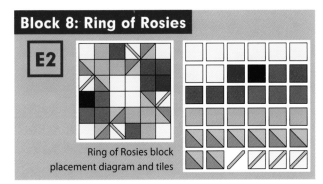

Ring of Rosies block placement diagram and tiles

Plain Big Tiles (24)

8 tiles of Fabric 1

6 tiles of Fabric 8

4 tiles of Fabric 6

3 tiles of Fabric 7

1 tile each of Fabric 2, Fabric 3, and Fabric 4

Half-square triangle Big Tiles (8)

8 tiles of Fabrics 5 and 9

Stem Big Tiles (background, stem, background) (4)

4 tiles of Fabrics 1, 9, and 1

Block 7: Ohio Ribbon Star

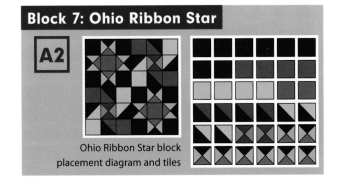

Ohio Ribbon Star block placement diagram and tiles

Plain Big Tiles (18)

8 tiles of Fabric 3

4 tiles each of Fabric 6 and Fabric 9

2 tiles of Fabric 4

Half-square triangle Big Tiles (8)

4 tiles each of Fabrics 3 and 6, and Fabrics 3 and 9

Quarter-square triangle Big Tiles (colors clockwise starting at top of tile) (10)

2 tiles of Fabrics 2, 5, 2, and 5

8 tiles of Fabrics 3, 8, 7, and 8

Block 9: Star in Boxes

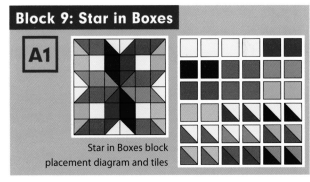

Star in Boxes block placement diagram and tiles

Plain Big Tiles (20)

4 tiles of Fabric 1

2 tiles each of Fabric 2, Fabric 3, Fabric 4, Fabric 5, Fabric 6, Fabric 7, Fabric 8, and Fabric 9

Half-square triangle Big Tiles (16)

2 tiles each of Fabrics 1 and 2, Fabrics 1 and 3, Fabrics 1 and 4, Fabrics 1 and 5, Fabrics 6 and 8, Fabrics 7 and 9, Fabrics 2 and 4, and Fabrics 3 and 5

Block 10: Darting Birds

B5

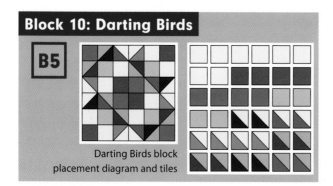

Darting Birds block placement diagram and tiles

Plain Big Tiles (20)

8 tiles of Fabric 1

4 tiles each of Fabric 6, Fabric 7, and Fabric 9

Half-square triangle Big Tiles (16)

4 tiles each of Fabrics 1 and 5, and Fabrics 2 and 8

2 tiles each of Fabrics 1 and 3, Fabrics 1 and 4, Fabrics 3 and 8, and Fabrics 4 and 8

Block 11: All Hallows

E1

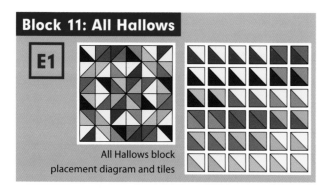

All Hallows block placement diagram and tiles

Half-square triangle Big Tiles (36)

4 tiles each of Fabrics 1 and 2, Fabrics 1 and 3, Fabrics 7 and 9, Fabrics 1 and 8, and Fabrics 1 and 9

2 tiles each of Fabrics 2 and 7, Fabrics 3 and 5, Fabrics 3 and 9, Fabrics 1 and 4, Fabrics 1 and 5, Fabrics 4 and 5, Fabrics 4 and 6, and Fabrics 6 and 8

Block 12: Pine Burr

C2

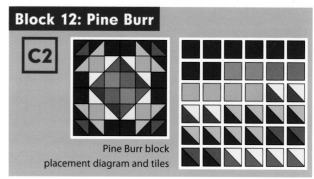

Pine Burr block placement diagram and tiles

Plain Big Tiles (16)

8 tiles of Fabric 3

4 tiles of Fabric 8

2 tiles each of Fabric 5 and Fabric 7

Half-square triangle Big Tiles (20)

8 tiles of Fabrics 3 and 9

4 tiles each of Fabrics 1 and 2, Fabrics 3 and 6, and Fabrics 1 and 4

Block 13: Double Ohio Star

C3

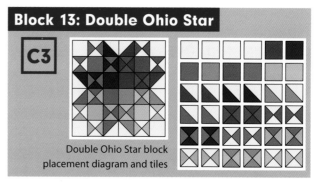

Double Ohio Star block placement diagram and tiles

Plain Big Tiles (12)

4 tiles of Fabric 1

1 tile each of Fabric 2, Fabric 3, Fabric 4, Fabric 5, Fabric 6, Fabric 7, Fabric 8, and Fabric 9

Half-square triangle Big Tiles (8)

2 tiles each of Fabrics 1 and 2, Fabrics 1 and 3, Fabrics 1 and 4, and Fabrics 1 and 5

Quarter-square triangle Big Tiles (colors clockwise starting at top of tile) (16)

2 tiles each of Fabrics 2, 6, 2, and 6; Fabrics 1, 6, 1, and 6; Fabrics 3, 7, 3, and 7; Fabrics 1, 7, 1, and 7; Fabrics 4, 8, 4, and 8; Fabrics 1, 8, 1, and 8; Fabrics 5, 9, 5, and 9; and Fabrics 1, 9, 1, and 9

Block 14: Barnraising

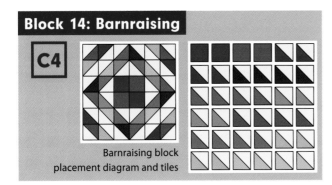

C4

Barnraising block placement diagram and tiles

Plain Big Tiles (4)

2 tiles each of Fabric 2 and Fabric 6

Half-square triangle Big Tiles (32)

4 tiles each of Fabrics 1 and 2, Fabrics 1 and 3, Fabrics 1 and 4, Fabrics 1 and 5, Fabrics 1 and 6, Fabrics 1 and 7, Fabrics 1 and 8, and Fabrics 1 and 9

Block 16: Woven Stars

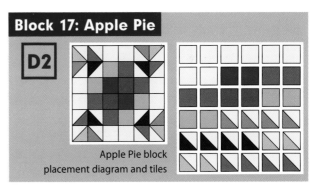

D1

Woven Stars block placement diagram and tiles

Plain Big Tiles (4)

1 tile each of Fabric 6, Fabric 7, Fabric 8, and Fabric 9

Half-square triangle Big Tiles (16)

3 tiles each of Fabrics 1 and 6, Fabrics 1 and 7, Fabrics 1 and 8, and Fabrics 1 and 9

1 tile each of Fabrics 4 and 6, Fabrics 5 and 7, Fabrics 4 and 8, and Fabrics 3 and 9

Half- and quarter-square triangle Big Tiles (colors clockwise starting at top of tile: quarter, half, quarter) (16)

4 tiles each of Fabrics 1, 5, and 2; Fabrics 1, 2, and 3; Fabrics 1, 4, and 5; and Fabrics 1, 3, and 4

Block 15: Formation Flying

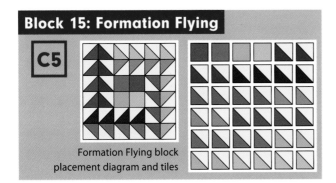

C5

Formation Flying block placement diagram and tiles

Plain Big Tiles (4)

1 tile each of Fabric 6, Fabric 7, Fabric 8, and Fabric 9

Half-square triangle Big Tiles (32)

4 tiles each of Fabrics 1 and 2, Fabrics 1 and 3, Fabrics 1 and 4, Fabrics 1 and 5, Fabrics 1 and 6, Fabrics 1 and 7, Fabrics 1 and 8, and Fabrics 1 and 9

Block 17: Apple Pie

D2

Apple Pie block placement diagram and tiles

Plain Big Tiles (20)

8 tiles of Fabric 1

2 tiles each of Fabric 2 and Fabric 6

4 tiles each of Fabric 4 and Fabric 8

Half-square triangle Big Tiles (16)

4 tiles each of Fabrics 1 and 3, Fabrics 1 and 5, Fabrics 1 and 7, and Fabrics 1 and 9

Block 18: Fun Fair

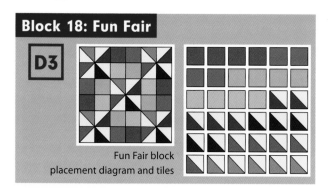

D3

Fun Fair block placement diagram and tiles

Plain Big Tiles (16)

4 tiles each of Fabric 6, Fabric 7, Fabric 8, and Fabric 9

Half-square triangle Big Tiles (20)

5 tiles each of Fabrics 1 and 2, Fabrics 1 and 3, Fabrics 1 and 4, and Fabrics 1 and 5

Block 20: Four Maple Leaves

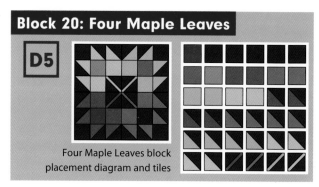

D5

Four Maple Leaves block placement diagram and tiles

Plain Big Tiles (16)

5 tiles of Fabric 3

2 tiles each of Fabric 6, Fabric 7, Fabric 8, and Fabric 9

1 tile each of Fabric 2, Fabric 4, and Fabric 5

Half-square triangle Big Tiles (16)

4 tiles each of Fabrics 3 and 6, Fabrics 3 and 7, Fabrics 3 and 8, and Fabrics 3 and 9

Stem Big Tiles (background, stem, background) (4)

1 tile each of Fabrics 3, 6, and 3; Fabrics 3, 7, and 3; Fabrics 3, 8, and 3; and Fabrics 3, 9, and 3

Block 19: Rail Fence

D4

Rail Fence block placement diagram and tiles

Half-square rectangle Big Tiles (36)

6 tiles of Fabrics 1 and 2

5 tiles each of Fabrics 1 and 4, and Fabrics 1 and 6

4 tiles each of Fabrics 1 and 3, Fabrics 1 and 5, Fabrics 1 and 7, Fabrics 1 and 8, and Fabrics 1 and 9

Block 21: Rambling Roses

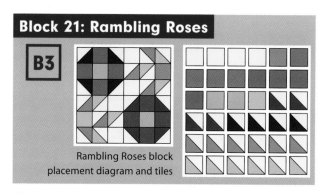

B3

Rambling Roses block placement diagram and tiles

Plain Big Tiles (16)

4 tiles each of Fabric 1, Fabric 6, and Fabric 7

2 tiles of Fabric 8

1 tile each of Fabric 9 and Fabric 5

Half-square triangle Big Tiles (20)

4 tiles each of Fabrics 1 and 2, and Fabrics 1 and 3

6 tiles each of Fabrics 1 and 5, and Fabrics 1 and 9

22: Holes in the Barn Door

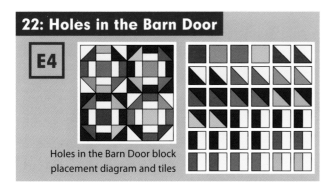

E4

Holes in the Barn Door block placement diagram and tiles

Plain Big Tiles (4)

1 tile each of Fabric 2, Fabric 5, Fabric 7, and Fabric 9

Half-square triangle Big Tiles (16)

2 tiles each of Fabrics 1 and 2, Fabrics 1 and 3, Fabrics 1 and 4, Fabrics 1 and 5, Fabrics 3 and 6, Fabrics 3 and 7, Fabrics 3 and 8, and Fabrics 3 and 9

Half-square rectangle Big Tiles (16)

8 tiles of Fabrics 1 and 3

4 tiles of Fabrics 1 and 6

2 tiles each of Fabrics 1 and 7, and Fabrics 1 and 8

Block 24: Hidden Stars

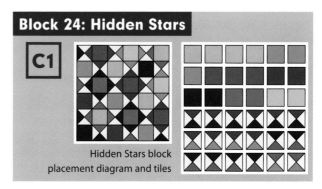

C1

Hidden Stars block placement diagram and tiles

Plain Big Tiles (18)

4 tiles of Fabric 8

3 tiles each of Fabric 5 and Fabric 6

2 tiles each of Fabric 2, Fabric 3, Fabric 7, and Fabric 9

Quarter-square triangle Big Tiles (colors clockwise starting at top of tile) (18)

6 tiles each of Fabrics 2, 1, 3, and 1; and Fabrics 3, 1, 4, and 1

4 tiles of Fabrics 2, 1, 5, and 1

2 tiles of Fabrics 4, 1, 5, and 1

Block 23: Egocentric

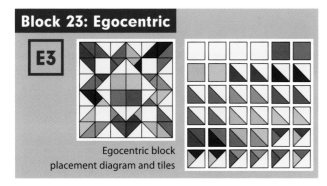

E3

Egocentric block placement diagram and tiles

Plain Big Tiles (8)

4 tiles of Fabric 1

1 tile each of Fabric 6, Fabric 7, Fabric 8, and Fabric 9

Half-square triangle Big Tiles (20)

1 tile each of Fabrics 2 and 6, Fabrics 3 and 7, Fabrics 4 and 8, and Fabrics 5 and 9

2 tiles each of Fabrics 1 and 2, Fabrics 1 and 3, Fabrics 1 and 4, Fabrics 1 and 5, Fabrics 1 and 6, Fabrics 1 and 7, Fabrics 1 and 8, and Fabrics 1 and 9

Half- and quarter-square triangle Big Tiles (colors clockwise starting at top of tile: quarter, half, quarter) (8)

1 tile each of Fabrics 2, 1, and 7; Fabrics 2, 1, and 8; Fabrics 3, 1, and 8; Fabrics 3, 1, and 9; Fabrics 5, 1, and 6; Fabrics 5, 1, and 7; Fabrics 4, 1, and 6; and Fabrics 4, 1, and 9

Block 25: Beverly

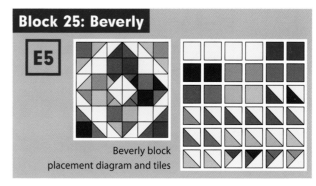

E5

Beverly block placement diagram and tiles

Plain Big Tiles (16)

4 tiles of Fabric 1

2 tiles each of Fabric 2, Fabric 3, Fabric 4, and Fabric 5

1 tile each of Fabric 6, Fabric 7, Fabric 8, and Fabric 9

Half-square triangle Big Tiles (16)

3 tiles each of Fabrics 1 and 6, Fabrics 1 and 7, Fabrics 1 and 8, and Fabrics 1 and 9

1 tile each of Fabrics 1 and 2, Fabrics 1 and 3, Fabrics 1 and 4, and Fabrics 1 and 5

Half- and quarter-square triangle Big Tiles (colors clockwise starting at top of tile: quarter, half, quarter) (4)

1 tile each of Fabrics 2, 1, and 9; Fabrics 3, 1, and 6; Fabrics 4, 1, and 7; and Fabrics 5, 1, and 8

Block 26: Sparkle

F1

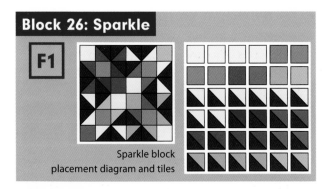

Sparkle block
placement diagram and tiles

Plain Big Tiles (12)

4 tiles each of Fabric 1 and Fabric 5

1 tile each of Fabric 6, Fabric 7, Fabric 8, and Fabric 9

Half-square triangle Big Tiles (24)

8 tiles of Fabrics 1 and 3

4 tiles each of Fabrics 6 and 3, and Fabrics 8 and 3

2 tiles each of Fabrics 2 and 3, Fabrics 4 and 3, Fabrics 7 and 3, and Fabrics 9 and 3

Block 27: Every Which Way but Loose

F2

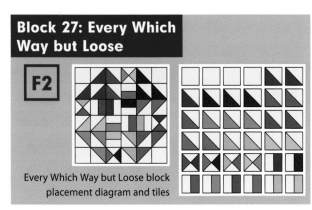

Every Which Way but Loose block
placement diagram and tiles

Plain Big Tiles (4)

4 tiles of Fabric 1

Half-square triangle Big Tiles (20)

3 tiles each of Fabrics 1 and 2, Fabrics 1 and 3, Fabrics 1 and 4, and Fabrics 1 and 5

2 tiles each of Fabrics 1 and 6, Fabrics 1 and 7, Fabrics 1 and 8, and Fabrics 1 and 9

Quarter-square triangle Big Tiles (colors clockwise starting at top of tile) (4)

1 tile each of Fabrics 1, 2, 1, and 6; Fabrics 1, 3, 1, and 7; Fabrics 1, 4, 1, and 8; and Fabrics 1, 5, 1, and 9

Half-square rectangle Big Tiles (8)

1 tile each of Fabrics 1 and 2, Fabrics 1 and 3, Fabrics 1 and 4, Fabrics 1 and 5, Fabrics 1 and 6, Fabrics 1 and 7, Fabrics 1 and 8, and Fabrics 1 and 9

Block 28: Card Trick Partners

F4

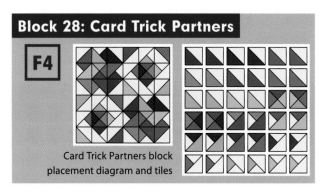

Card Trick Partners block
placement diagram and tiles

Half-square triangle Big Tiles (16)

2 tiles each of Fabrics 1 and 2, Fabrics 1 and 3, Fabrics 1 and 4, Fabrics 1 and 5, Fabrics 1 and 6, Fabrics 1 and 7, Fabrics 1 and 8, and Fabrics 1 and 9

Quarter-square triangle Big Tiles (colors clockwise starting at top of tile) (4)

1 tile each of Fabrics 6, 9, 8, and 7; and Fabrics 6, 7, 8, and 9

2 tiles of Fabrics 6, 3, 4, and 5

Half- and quarter-square triangle Big Tiles (colors clockwise starting at top of tile: quarter, half, quarter) (16)

2 tiles each of Fabrics 5, 6, and 1; Fabrics 4, 9, and 1; Fabrics 3, 8, and 1; Fabrics 2, 7, and 1; Fabrics 1, 1, and 2; Fabrics 1, 1, and 7; Fabrics 1, 1, and 8; and Fabrics 1, 1, and 9

Block 29: Spinners

F3

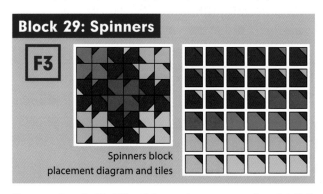

Spinners block
placement diagram and tiles

Corner triangle Big Tiles (big section, corner triangle) (36)

8 tiles of Fabrics 8 and 3

4 tiles each of Fabrics 3 and 6, Fabrics 3 and 7, Fabrics 3 and 8, Fabrics 3 and 9, Fabrics 6 and 3, Fabrics 7 and 3, and Fabrics 9 and 3

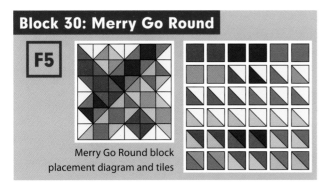

Block 30: Merry Go Round

F5

Merry Go Round block placement diagram and tiles

Plain Big Tiles (8)

2 tiles each of Fabric 2, Fabric 3, Fabric 4, and Fabric 5

Half-square triangle Big Tiles (28)

3 tiles each of Fabrics 1 and 6, Fabrics 1 and 7, Fabrics 1 and 8, and Fabrics 1 and 9

2 tiles each of Fabrics 2 and 8, Fabrics 3 and 6, Fabrics 4 and 9, Fabrics 5 and 7, Fabrics 6 and 9, and Fabrics 7 and 8

1 tile each of Fabrics 1 and 2, Fabrics 1 and 3, Fabrics 1 and 4, and Fabrics 1 and 5

Quilt instruction steps continued from page 55.

2. Add sashing to the blocks.

Piece the 1½″ × width of fabric strips of tan and darkest green fabrics together lengthwise; then cut 71 pieces 1½″ × 6½″ for sashing posts and 84 segments 1½″ × 1½″ for four-patch corners.

Make 21 four-patches 2½″ × 2½″, and 21 reversed four-patches 2½″ × 2½″.

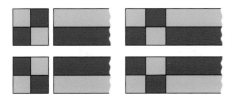

Sashing posts and corners

Referring to the quilt layout diagram (below), stitch the four-patches, reversed four-patches, and sashing posts together in rows. Stitch the vertical sashing to the blocks. Press. Join the blocks in rows. Press. Stitch the blocks and sashing together in rows. Press.

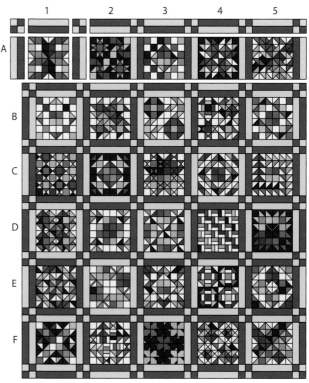

Quilt layout diagram

3. Quilt and bind.

Referring to Quilting Mini-Mosaics (page 18), layer, baste, and quilt as desired. Referring to Binding (page 18), join the 2½″ × width of fabric strips of binding together and bind the quilt.

projects continued

RAMBLING ROSE HANDBAG
(continued from page 26)

5. Make the exterior panel.

Cut the 2″ × width of fabric and the 6½″ × width of fabric strips of Fabric 9 to the same length as the panel (33½″ in sample). With right sides together, stitch the 2″-wide strip to the top of the panel, and the 6½″-wide strip to the bottom of the panel. The bag exterior measures 14½″ × 33½″.

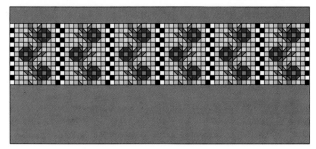

Rambling Rose Handbag exterior panel

Cut a 14″-wide strip of fusible fleece to measure 33″ long and fuse it to the wrong side of the panel, leaving a ¼″ seam allowance of fabric exposed around the fusible fleece. Machine quilt the panel as desired.

6. Prepare the interior pockets.

Cut the 11″ × width of fabric piece of Fabric 11 to the same length as the exterior bag panel (33½″). Cut the 5″-wide piece of fusible fleece to measure 33″ long. Fold and press the 11″ × 33½″ piece of Fabric 11 in half lengthwise, right side out. Open the folded fabric and align the fusible fleece with the fold line, leaving a ¼″ seam allowance exposed on either end. Refold the fabric and fuse the fleece. Stitch ¼″ from the fold through all 3 thicknesses.

7. Prepare the bag lining.

Cut the 14½″ × width of fabric strip of Fabric 10 to the same length as the exterior bag panel (33½″). Cut the remaining 14″-wide piece of fusible fleece to measure 33″ long and fuse it to the wrong side of the 14½″ × 33½″ piece of Fabric 10. Leave a clear ¼″ seam allowance exposed around the fusible fleece. Quilt as desired.

8. Stitch pocket section to bag lining.

Using a ruler and pen or pencil, mark a line on the right side of the bag lining 4½″ from and parallel to the long raw bottom edge. With the pocket section fold pointing downward, align the raw edges of the pocket section with this marked line, and pin to hold in place. Stitch the pocket section onto the lining section ¼″ from the raw edge of the pocket section. Turn the pocket section up and top-stitch along the length of the pocket section bottom ¼″ in from the seam.

Fold the lining section in half (aligning the short edges) and mark the halfway line with chalk or a removable marker. On the right side of the pocket section mark a line 2½″ from the halfway line on both sides. Also mark a line across the pocket section 2¾″ from the outside raw edges. Stitch along these lines through all thicknesses to form the side pockets. Start each of the seams with a backstitch or about ¼″ of small zigzag stitching to reinforce the tops of the pockets. Stitch as many other pockets as you desire along the 2 long parts of the pocket section. Most people find it handy to have a pocket big enough to fit their wallet, another for a cell phone, and so on.

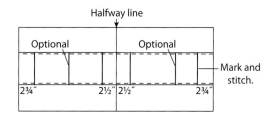

Rambling Rose Handbag lining panel diagram

9. Make the bag straps.

Center a 3″ strip of stiff fusible interfacing on the wrong side of each 4¼″ strip of Fabric 9. Fold the long raw fabric edges around the interfacing strip and then fold the unit in half lengthwise, wrong sides together. Press and top-stitch the edges to make 2 bag straps. Topstitch the bag straps lengthwise several more times as desired. From each strap cut 2 pieces 3″ long. Insert these 4 pieces into the 4 D-rings or flat rectangle rings. Stitch as close as possible to the edge of the rings through the 2 thicknesses of the strap bits.

10. Make the side ties, button loop, and optional key loop.

Fold and press the lengthwise raw edges of the 3 Fabric 9 strips 1¼″ × width of fabric in toward the center of the strip; then fold and press in half again. Stitch the folded edges together. Stitch along the entire length of the ties again with a decorative stitch in a contrasting thread if desired. From these, cut 2 pieces 36″ long for the side ties, 1 piece 8″ long for the button loop, and 1 piece 12″ long for the optional key loop.

11. Assemble the bag.

Pin, then stitch, the 4 D-ring sections of the bag straps and button loop along the top raw edge of the right side of the exterior bag piece with raw edges of about ½″ above the bag section raw edge and with the D-rings and loop pointing downward.

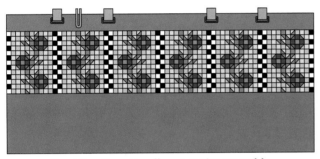

Rambling Rose Handbag exterior assembly showing D-ring and button loop

12. Tie the bolt snap or key ring to the center of the 12″-long key loop piece; then pin and stitch the 2 loose tie ends 4″ down from the top raw edge along a short side of the bag lining.

13. Fold both the bag lining and exterior pieces in half, parallel to the short edges, with right sides facing inward. (The key loop piece lies between the right sides.) Pin and stitch the side and bottom seams, using a ¼″ seam allowance and leaving an 8″ opening at the center bottom of the bag lining.

14. Line up the 2½″ × 2½″ template with the seamlines at the bottom corners of the lining and exterior pieces. Trace around the template with a marking pen. Repeat the markings on the other side of both bag pieces.

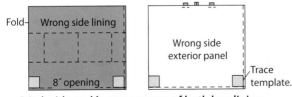

Stitch side and bottom seams of both bag lining and exterior panels, and mark corners.

15. With right sides together, squish the corners flat, lining up the side folds or seams with the bottom seam. Pin, then stitch and backstitch, along the resulting straight line across each bottom corner of both bag pieces. Trim away the excess fabric from the corners ¼″ away from seam.

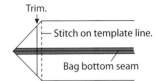

Stitch bottom corners of bag lining and exterior panel.

16. Attach the bag feet through the plastic canvas bag bottom, as follows.

Cut a small piece from each of the 4 corners of the 4½″ × 11″ rectangle of plastic canvas, so there are no sharp, pointy corners to work their way through the fabric of the bag. Mark, then snip out, 4 holes in the plastic canvas, approximately 1½″ from the short side and 1″ from the long side at the 4 corners of the rectangle. Center the plastic canvas along the flat bottom of the wrong side of the bag exterior and make a mark through the holes to position the bag feet. Use a tailor's awl or large needle to poke a hole through the fleece and fabric. Insert a bag foot through each hole in the fabric and the corresponding hole in the plastic canvas; then open and flatten the wings of each bag foot.

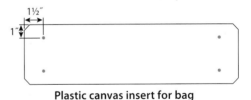

Plastic canvas insert for bag

17. Stitch the bag together.

Keep the bag exterior with the right side facing inward. Turn the bag lining right side out; then insert it into the bag exterior, making sure to have a single side seam on each side of the bag (the lining seam at one end and the bag seam at the other). Pin, then stitch, the bag tops together, using a ¼″ seam allowance. Take your time with this step, use a walking foot, and use a slightly longer stitch and a larger needle if you find the going tough. Carefully pull the bag through the 8″ opening in the bottom of the lining piece; then insert the bag lining into the bag exterior. Make sure the top seam is well turned out. Pin and then topstitch ¼″ away from the seam.

18. Position the side ties so that the bottom edge of the tie is lined up on the seam where the narrow top border of Fabric 9 meets the Rambling Rose panel at the sides of the bag. Stitch the side ties onto the bag through all the thicknesses so that the center 5″ of each tie is sewn centrally onto both sides of the bag.

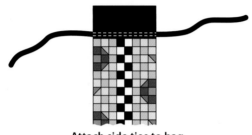

Attach side ties to bag.

19. Hand stitch closed the opening that was left at the bottom of the bag lining.

20. Attach the straps by inserting each end of the 2 straps through the D-rings and turning up about 1½″ of the strap. Stitch to secure using a straight stitch and then again using a zigzag stitch to cover the raw edge.

21. Cover the 10½″ × 4″ piece of foam core board with the remnant of batting and glue into place. Fold and press the 9½″ × 12″ piece of Fabric 11 in half along the length, and stitch 2 sides to make a "pillowcase" measuring about 4¾″ × 12″. Insert the foam core board and stitch the remaining side closed by hand. Insert this into the bag bottom.

22. Stitch on the button and tie the side ties into a bow. If desired, slip a Pandora-style decorative bead over each end of the side ties and secure with a knot.

ZIGZAG WALLET
(continued from page 28)

3. Make the wallet.

Sandwich the Zigzag panel with the 7″ × 11″ piece of batting and the 7″ × 11″ piece of Fabric 3. Staystitch ⅛″ in from the raw edge of the Mini-Mosaic panel; then machine quilt the 3 layers as desired. After quilting, trace around the edges of Template A (at right) ⅛″ in from the panel raw edge to round off the corners at one end of the

wallet. Use the walking foot on your machine to stitch on the marked line through all thicknesses. Trim the lining fabric and batting to ¼″ outside of the stitching line. There should be about ⅛″ of exposed batting and lining around the edges of the Mini-Mosaic panel.

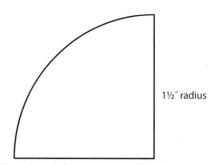

1½″ radius

Template A for rounding off wallet corners

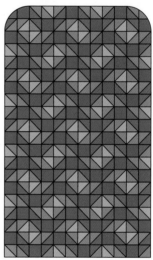

Round off 2 corners of wallet panel.

4. Make a 2½″-wide continuous bias tape from the 15″ × 15″ square of Fabric 5. The 15″ × 15″ square will yield about 80″ of 2½″-wide bias tape. To make bias binding, fold and press the bias tape in half lengthwise, right sides out, so that the 2 long raw edges meet.

5. Prepare the Quilter's Vinyl ID card insert, as follows:

Cut a 4″-long piece of bias binding and stitch it to a 3½″ side of the Quilter's Vinyl piece. Align the raw edges of the bias binding to the cut edge of the Quilter's Vinyl and stitch using a ⅜″ seam allowance. Bring the folded edge of the bias binding around to cover the seam. Pin and topstitch close to the inner folded edge of the binding, about ⅜″ from the outer edge. Trim the side edges even so that the piece measures 3½″ × 4½″.

TIP

You may find it easier to machine stitch on the Quilter's Vinyl if you cover it with tissue paper before sewing.

6. Make the ID and credit card section.

Measure, mark, fold accordion style, and press; then stitch pleats into the 3½″ × width of fabric strip of Fabric 3. Stitch ⅛″ in from the surface pleat fold lines and stitch ⅛″ from the furthest interior pleat on the left, through the top layer of fabric.

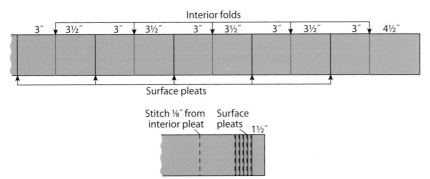

Pleat credit card section of wallet.

7. Place the prepared Quilter's Vinyl piece so that the bound edge is close to the edge of the first pleat on the left. Use a straight stitch on the machine to staystitch the Quilter's Vinyl and pleats in place ⅛″ from the outer raw edges. Trim away the excess fabric so the section measures 3½″ × 7½″.

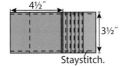

Bound edge of ID card insert near first pleat

8. Line the credit card section and add the hook and loop tape closure.

Stitch the 5″ × 7½″ piece of Fabric 1, right sides together, to the top of the credit card section. Use a straight stitch and a ⅜″ seam allowance. Flip the fabric up and over the top of the credit card section to create a bound-edge look. Stitch along the seamline, in-the-ditch, using a straight stitch. Then staystitch along the bottom of the unit ⅛″ from the raw edge so that the credit card section is now lined. Trim any excess lining below the cardholder.

Position, center, and staystitch the sides of the credit card section on the inside of the wallet piece, 4″ from the bottom squared corners. Make sure that the last credit card pleat on the right is at least ½″ from the side edge of the wallet. Trim the credit card section to the size of the wallet. Center and stitch the loop part of the hook and loop tape closure to the wallet, about 1½″ from the inside top edge, and the hook piece on the outside of the wallet (on the pieced panel),

with the top edge 1½″ from the outside bottom edge. Trim the lining the size of the credit card section.

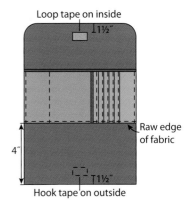

Attach credit card section and add hook and loop tape closure.

9. Make the bottom section of the coin purse.

Fold the 7½″ × 8″ piece of Fabric 1 in half, right sides out, to measure 7½″ × 4″. Insert a 3¾″ × 7″ piece of batting and align to the fold line. Use a straight stitch to topstitch ¼″ from the fold. Center and stitch on a small piece of hook and loop tape (loop side) about 1½″ in from the folded edge of the piece. Add quilting if desired.

10. Make the top flap of the coin purse.

Mark around Template B (page 68) on the wrong side of a 4″ × 7½″ piece of Fabric 2. Fuse or baste the remaining 3¾″ × 7″ piece of batting to the wrong side of the second 4″ × 7½″ piece of Fabric 2, leaving ¼″ of fabric exposed on the top and sides. Sandwich the marked fabric piece, right sides together, with the batted piece of fabric. Stitch along the curved edges and bottom only, leaving the top (longest) edge and the little short, straight sides open.

Zigzag Wallet

Template B

Coin Purse Flap

Template for Zigzag Wallet coin purse closure flap (includes ¼″ seam allowances)

11. Clip and notch the curves as needed and turn the top flap right side out. Topstitch ¼″ from the seam. With right sides together, align the top raw edges of the flap with the bottom raw edges of the credit card section. The flap points upward. Using a walking foot, stitch the open long edge of the top flap, through all thicknesses, to the bottom raw edge of the credit card section of the wallet. Flip the top flap down, away from the credit card section, and topstitch ¼″ away from the seam.

12. Staystitch the coin purse section.

Position the bottom section of the coin purse (from Step 9) so that the top folded edge comes right up to the edge of the top flap. Staystitch in place ⅛″ from the side raw edges of the wallet; then trim away the excess fabric. Position and stitch the final piece of hook and loop tape onto the bottom side of the top flap of the coin purse.

13. Bind with bias binding.

Bind the perimeter of the wallet with the bias binding. Apply the binding onto the exterior panel sides using a ⅜″ seam allowance. Bring the folded edge to the interior side and use a blind hem stitch to finish.

14. Stitch decorative buttons or yo-yos onto the wallet and coin purse closures to hide the hook and loop tape stitching, if desired.

TESS THE STARLET SEWING BOX
(continued from page 31)

3. Make the box.

Line up the 4 pieces 5″ × 12¾″ of mat board lengthwise. Glue them to each other using the 2″ × 4″ Fabric 10 hinges, creating 1 long foldable piece of mat board measuring about 51″ × 5″.

4. Spread the glue evenly over a surface of each of the mat board pieces from Step 3, and glue the pieces onto the 6″ × 54″ piece of batting. Allow the glue to dry and then trim away the excess batting around each piece.

Hinge and glue all box sides together.

5. Add the border to the Mini-Mosaic panel.

Stitch the 3″ × 10½″ pieces of Fabric 10 to opposite sides of the panel; then press the seam allowances away from the panel. Stitch the 3″ × 15½″ pieces of Fabric 10 to the remaining sides of the panel, so the panel measures 15½″ × 15½″. Press.

6. Spread glue evenly over the surface of the 13″ × 13″ piece of mat board and glue the piece onto the 14″ × 14″ batting. Trim the excess batting. Center the pieced fabric panel over the 13″ × 13″ piece of mat board, with the batting side next to the wrong side of the panel. Turn it over onto a flat working surface. Glue the fabric edges around the mat board to the back side, starting with the 2 seamed sides, and pull the fabric taut around the mat board.

> **TIP**
>
> After the first two sides have been glued down and have dried, trim away a small square of fabric from each folded end. This reduces the bulk and makes gluing the next two sides easier.

7. Cover the batting side of the long, hinged 5″ × 51″ mat board with the 7″-wide strip of Fabric 10, making sure to line up the seam with a hinge. Trim the fabric at the ends of the strip 1″ beyond the mat board. Cover the 12¾″ × 12¾″ piece of mat board with a 14″ × 14″ piece of batting. Trim the batting and cover with the 15″ × 15″ piece of Fabric 10. Glue the fabric edges to the back side of the mat board. Cover all of the remaining pieces of mat board with the pieces cut from Fabric 11 and a layer of batting.

8. Make interior pockets, as follows.

Fold and press under ¼″, then another ½″, along the long sides of a 6″ × 18″ rectangle of Fabric 11. Stitch next to the first fold to create a casing for the elastic. Cut a 24″-long piece of ¼″ elastic and thread it through the casing. Gather the pocket fabric toward the center of the elastic until it measures about 13″ wide; then staystitch through the fabric and the elastic to hold the gathers in place. Do not trim the ends of the elastic.

9. Stitch the raw ends of the elastic from Step 8 together to form a loop. Stretch the loop around a side piece of the 4¾″ × 12½″ interior mat board and lining, positioning the elastic gathering so that it is about ½″ from a long side and the fabric gathers wrap around the edges and bottom of the piece by about ½″. Glue the fabric edges in place on the back of the mat board.

Repeat Steps 8 and 9 to make the second pocket.

10. Center and glue all 4 of the inner box sides, mat board sides together, to the 4 hinged pieces of the outer box. Use clothespins or bulldog clips to hold the pieces together until the glue is dry.

11. Stitch the box sides to the box bottom, as follows.

Stitch the short ends of the box side panel together by hand with a ladder stitch, using a curved needle and hand quilting thread. Turn the box sides upside down onto a work surface. Pin the outside of the Fabric 10 box bottom in place at the corners with long straight pins; then use a curved needle and quilting thread to stitch it in place.

12. Turn the box right side up. Glue a 12½″ × 12½″ piece of mat/batting covered with Fabric 11 to the inside bottom of the box, wrong sides together. Weigh this down with a few food cans while the glue dries.

13. Make the button loops.

Fold each 1½″ × 9″ piece of Fabric 10 in half lengthwise with the right sides together. Stitch the raw edges together to make a tube. Turn the tubes right side out. Cut and insert a 6″-long piece of ¼″ elastic into each tube. Gather the fabric tubes as needed to expose ½″ of elastic at each end. Fold the loops in half, and then stitch across the ends to secure the fabric, making 4 flat loops.

Note: Align the elastic ends side by side. Do not overlap them.

14. Finish the box lid.

Glue the loops to the mat board side of the outer box lid 1″ from the corners on the front and back edges of the lid. Extend the loops 2″ beyond the edge of the lid.

15. Glue the second of the 12½″ × 12½″ pieces of mat/batting covered with Fabric 11 to the inside of the box lid. Secure with clothespins or bulldog clips until the glue is dry. Stitch the 4 buttons in place on the outside of the box to correspond with the loops.

DARTING BIRDS NECK ROLL CUSHION
(continued from page 33)

3. Stitch the 3 panels together using the 1½″-wide strips of Fabric 6 to create a 1″-wide sashing strip between the panels.

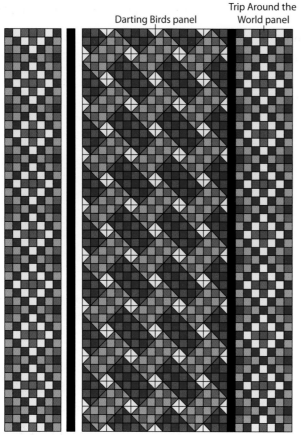

Darting Birds panel   Trip Around the World panel

Panel and sashing layout

4. Sandwich the panel, flannel, and backing fabric. Quilt as desired. Staystitch around the outer edge of the panel ⅛″ from the raw edges. At this stage, the quilt panel will measure 18½″ × 24½″.

5. Make the drawstring sections.

From the Fabric 6 strips 5″ × width of fabric, cut 2 pieces 5″ × 26″. Hem the short 5″ ends by folding under ½″ then another ½″. Press. Machine stitch the hem near the first fold. Each piece measures 5″ × 24″ at this point.

Fold and press ½″ and ½″ again on a 24″-long side of each of the 2 pieces. Cut the drawstring cord in half and insert the drawstring cord into the fold before stitching the hem. Stitch the hem, enclosing the cord. Use a safety pin to hold the cord in place while finishing the cushion cover.

Center and stitch the remaining 24″-long raw edge of the drawstring sections to the long sides of the Mini-Mosaic panel, *wrong sides together*, leaving ¼″ of the panel exposed at the top and bottom of the seam. Stitch using a ¼″ seam allowance. The raw edges of this seam will be on the right side of the project at this stage.

6. Finish the cushion cover.

Stitch the Mini-Mosaic panel into a tube, right sides together. (This seam is perpendicular to the seams stitched in Step 5.) After stitching, at the drawstring seams, clip the seam allowances just to the stitching, taking care not to clip the drawstring piece. Fold the clipped flaps to the right side of the drawstring section. Where the Mini-Mosaic panel connects with the drawstring sections, cover the raw seam allowances by binding the seams with the 2½″-wide Fabric 6 strips, folded in half lengthwise. Include the clipped flaps in the bound seam. Slipstitch the drawstring section together at the 2 short, hemmed ends up to the drawstring casing.

Insert the cushion form, batting roll, or other stuffing. Pull and tie the drawstring cord ends into a bow. Add beads or knots to the cord ends if desired.

SHOWTIME BADGE BAG
(continued from page 36)

3. Make the bias binding.

Make a 2½″-wide continuous bias tape using the 15″ × 15″ square of Fabric 16 (it will yield about 80″ of bias tape at this width). Fold and press the bias tape in half lengthwise with the raw edges together and the right side outward.

4. Make the bag exterior.

Use a pencil and a ruler to draw a 2½″ × 2½″ square in the center of the paper side of the 3½″ × 3½″ piece of fusible web. Position and fuse the fusible web square onto the wrong side of a 6″ × 18¼″ piece of Fabric 15, 1″ from the top raw edge and centered so that 1¼″ of Fabric 15 is left exposed on each side of the fusible web square. Cut out the 2½″ center square of fusible web and fabric, and discard. Remove the paper backing from the remaining fusible web. Clip interior corners of the square up to the edge of the fusible web; then fold and fuse to the wrong side to create a 3½″ × 3½″ opening.

5. Working from the right side of the bag front, center the Bear's Paw block behind the opening and pin it in place. Use invisible thread on the top of your machine, and use a narrow zigzag stitch around the inner perimeter of the cut-out square to hold the Mini-Mosaic in place permanently. Fuse the wrong side of the bag front to a 5½″ × 17¾″ piece of fast2fuse, leaving a ¼″ seam allowance around the perimeter.

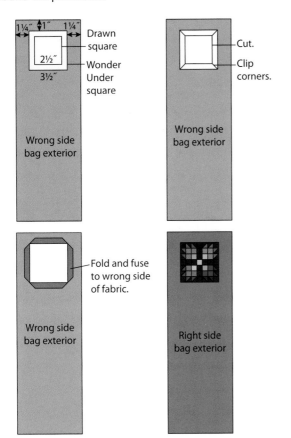

Inset Bear's Paw block into bag front fabric.

6. Make the show badge and passport pockets.

Cut 2 pieces of the bias binding, each 6½″ long. Stitch onto the 2 short sides of the 6″ × 11″ rectangle of Quilter's Vinyl using a ⅜″ seam allowance. Bring the folded edge of the bias binding over the edge of the Quilter's Vinyl. Machine topstitch in place.

7. Make the business card pocket.

Fold, then press, the 6″ × 10″ piece of Fabric 15 in half, right sides of fabric out, so the pocket measures 6″ × 5″.

Open the fabric piece. Line up and fuse the 5½″ side of the remaining fusible web rectangle to the wrong side of the folded pocket with an edge along the fold line, leaving a ¼″ seam allowance on the other 3 sides. Remove the paper backing and fuse the wrong sides of the fabric pocket together. Machine topstitch ¼″ in from the folded edge.

8. Stitch the exterior pockets in place.

Align one bound top edge of the Quilter's Vinyl pocket 5½″ from the top edge of the front bag exterior piece, (slightly below the Mini-Mosaic panel). To create a pen pocket next to the passport pocket, stitch a straight line 1¼″ in from the raw edge on a side of the large section of the Quilter's Vinyl. Position and pin the lower raw edges of the business card pocket 3¼″ from the bound edge of the Quilter's Vinyl piece, with the folded edge of the pocket pointed toward the top Mini-Mosaic end of the bag exterior. Stitch through all thicknesses ¼″ from the raw edge of the bottom pocket.

Fold the business card pocket over; then topstitch a parallel line through all thicknesses ¼″ from the seamline. Staystitch all pockets in place ⅛″ from the bag sides. Trim away excess bias binding.

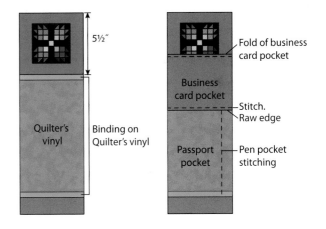

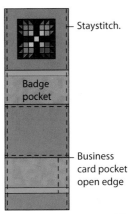

Showtime Badge Bag front assembly

9. Make the bag interior.

Fuse the remaining 5½″ × 18″ piece of fast2fuse to the remaining 6″ × 18½″ piece of Fabric 15, leaving a ¼″ seam allowance all around.

10. Make the glasses and cell phone pockets.

Fold under ½″ of a long side of the 6½″ × 8″ piece of Fabric 4; then fold in ½″ again, so the piece measures 5½″ × 8″. Stitch along the edge of the first fold to create a casing for ¼″ elastic. Insert a 7″ piece of black elastic into the casing and gather the fabric so that ½″ of elastic is exposed at both ends. Staystitch the elastic in place. At the opposite end of the pocket make a double pleat at the center and a small pleat ¾″ in from each corner, so that the overall pocket measures 5½″ × 6″. Staystitch the pleats in place ⅛″ from the folded edges of the pleats for an inch or so.

11. Stitch the pleated end of the pocket to the bag interior base.

Cut 2 pieces of ¼″ black elastic, each about 4″ long, to make interior loops. Staystitch the ends of each loop, 4″ apart, to the bottom pleated edge of the pocket. Draw a line 6½″ from one short end of the interior base. Line up the pleated lower edge of the pocket to the drawn line, right sides of fabric together. Stitch across the bottom of the pocket. Flip pocket up and topstitch ¼″ from the seam. Topstitch the pocket down the center to create 2 compartments. Staystitch the sides of the pockets to the interior base using a ⅛″ seam allowance.

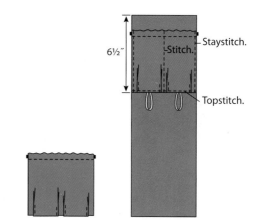

Make inside glasses and cell phone pockets.

12. Make the fastening flaps.

Trace and cut out the flap template (below) onto the template plastic. Trace and cut 2 pieces of fast2fuse the exact size of the template. Trace around the template onto the wrong side of 2 pieces 2½″ × 5″ of Fabric 10, leaving a ¼″ seam allowance all around. Position the fast2fuse pieces inside the marked lines on the fabric. Fuse in place. Sandwich each flap, right sides together, with the remaining pieces of Fabric 10. Stitch along the curved edge of the fast2fuse, leaving the long straight side of the flap open. Turn the flaps right side out and press. Stitch a small ¾″ loop piece of hook and loop tape at the center of the long curved side, ⅛″ in from the edge.

Flap
Showtime Badge Bag

Flap template for coin purse and tissue holder for Showtime Badge Bag

13. Make the upper interior pocket.

Fold the 7″ × 8″ piece of Fabric 7 in half, right sides together, to measure 7″ × 4″. Stitch along the short ends. *Center* and press the 4½″ × 3½″ piece of fast2fuse to a pocket side, just inside the fabric fold, leaving about a ¼″ seam allowance of fabric free at the open end of the pocket (the 4½″ edge of the fast2fuse is parallel to the 7″ edge of the folded pocket). Turn the pocket right side out. Press. Center and stitch a small ¾″ hook piece of hook and loop tape about ½″ from the top folded edge of the pocket. Position the pocket top 1″ from the top edge of the interior bag (at the opposite end from the glasses and cell phone pockets). Pin the pocket sides 1″ from the sides of the bag interior and topstitch the pocket in place along the sides of the pocket only. Make a small ½" pleat at each bottom pocket corner; then staystitch along the bottom edge of the pocket.

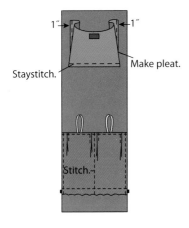

14. Make the tissue holder.

Fold and press the 5" × 6½" piece of Fabric 5 in half, right sides together, to measure 5" × 3¼". Stitch the 2 short sides. Turn the tissue holder right side out. Insert the 3" × 4½" piece of fast2fuse in place along the fold. Press, leaving a ¼" seam allowance free along the open end. Center and stitch a ¾" hook piece of hook and loop tape about ½" from the folded top edge. Mark a line 8¼" from the top of the bag interior (at the end opposite the glasses pocket). Place the raw edges of the tissue holder along this line, right sides together. Stitch over the opening through all thicknesses using a ¼" seam allowance, and then flip the tissue holder up toward the purse pocket and topstitch ¼" from the seam.

15. Stitch on the flaps.

With right sides together, align the raw edges of the tissue holder flap with the purse pocket bottom. Stitch in place through all thicknesses and then flip it down over the tissue holder and topstitch ¼" from the

seam. With right sides together, align the raw edges of the purse pocket flap with the center top of the bag interior. Staystitch in position ⅛" in from the raw edge.

Stitch purse pocket and tissue holder to Showtime Badge Bag interior and add flaps.

16. Make the bag sides.

Make the D-ring sections. Slip the 2"-long pieces of grosgrain ribbon through the D-rings, and stitch through the ribbon as close to the D-ring as possible. Fold and press the 4 pieces 3½" × 8½" of Fabric 15 in half lengthwise, right sides together, so each measures 1¾" × 8½". Pin each of the D-rings inside 2 of the pieces of folded fabric.

17. Make the bag side sections.

Stitch the 2 short sides of all 4 folded pieces with a ¼" seam allowance. Turn the pieces right side out. Insert, then press, a 1½" × 8" piece of fast2fuse into each piece. Stitch the 2 hook pieces of the 7¾" hook and loop tape pieces to the outsides of the 2 side sections with D-rings. Stitch the 2 loop pieces to the insides of the other 2 side pieces.

Stitch hook pieces to D-ring sections.

Stitch loop pieces to plain sides.

Make bag sides with D-rings and hook and loop tape.

18. Stitch the sides onto the inner bag panel; then stitch the inner and outer bag pieces together. Position the bag sides ½" from the short ends of the interior bag piece.

Staystitch the 2 bag sides without the D-rings onto the purse and tissue holder section, with the loop tape side down. Staystitch the 2 bag sides with D-rings to the glasses and cell phone pocket section, with the hook tape side up.

19. Stitch the bag exterior to the bag interior. Use a ¼" seam on all of the raw edges. Stitch 2 lines at the bag base through all thicknesses.

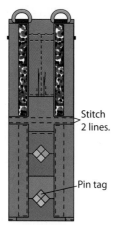

Stitch
2 lines.

Pin tag

Stitch Showtime Badge Bag side and interior pieces together.

Bind the raw edges. Stitch the 2½˝-wide bias binding of Fabric 16 using a ⅜˝ seam. Apply the bias onto the exterior bag and miter the corners. Bring the folded bias edge to the bag interior and hem by hand. Stitch the bottoms of the bag sides with D-rings to the bottom of the bag by hand.

20. Make the pin tags and add the neck chain.

Make 8 pin tags by making 16 four-patches from the 1˝ × 1˝ squares of Fabrics 2, 3, 9, and 12 (see Making Four-Patch Big Tiles, page 11). Fuse these to both sides of the 8 squares 1½˝ × 1½˝ of fast2fuse. Zigzag stitch around the pin tag raw edges. Stitch 2 pin tags to the interior bag flaps to conceal the hook and loop tape. Stitch a small jump ring onto 1 corner of each of the remaining 6 pin tags for attaching to the neck chain.

Cut the bag chain to the desired length and attach the ends to the 2 D-rings. Attach the pin tags to the chain to finish the bag.

TIP

If desired, a tube of fabric can be used instead of a chain. In the sample, pony beads were used both inside and outside the fabric tube.

OHIO RIBBON STAR CUSHION COVER
(continued from page 38)

3. Make the cushion cover front. Refer to the cushion cover front diagram (page 38). Cut each of the 2˝ × width of fabric border strips of Fabric 2 into 2 pieces: 2˝ × 15½˝ and 2˝ × 18½˝. Add the borders to the Ohio Ribbon Star Mini-Mosaic panel, sewing the shorter strips to the top and

bottom and the longer strips to the sides. Press as you go. The panel, with the border, measures 18½˝ × 18½˝.

Sandwich the bordered panel with the 20˝ × 20˝ piece of flannel or thin batting and the 20˝ × 20˝ piece of muslin; baste and machine quilt as desired. Staystitch around the panel ⅛˝ from the raw edge, and trim away the excess batting and muslin.

4. Make the overlapping cushion cover back.

With right sides together, stitch each 13˝ × 20˝ piece of Fabric 2 to a 10˝ × 20˝ piece of muslin along their long edges. Press the seam allowances toward Fabric 2; then fold and press both units in half, right sides out, so they each measure 11¼˝ × 20˝. Insert a batting piece 11˝ × 20˝ inside, up to the fold line. Stitch 1˝ away from the fold line. Baste and machine quilt both pieces as desired.

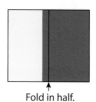

Fold in half.

Make 2 for overlapping cushion back.

Fold a 20˝ cushion back piece crosswise to find the halfway point; then stitch a buttonhole about 1˝ in from the long folded edge. Overlap the long folded edges of both pieces by about 4˝ so that together they measure 18½˝ × 20˝. Staystitch ⅛˝ from the edges along the overlap.

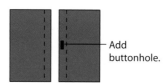

Add buttonhole.

Make buttonhole on backing piece.

5. Assemble the cushion cover.

Pin, then stitch, the front Ohio Ribbon Star panel to the overlapped cushion back, wrong sides together. Trim away the excess cushion back.

Make the binding by stitching the 2½˝ × width of fabric strips of Fabric 2 together at their short ends with a 45° seam. Fold the strip in half lengthwise, right sides out. Stitch the binding around the raw edges of the cushion cover; and then turn the folded edge to the back and stitch in place. Stitch a button to correspond to the buttonhole. Insert the 18˝ × 18˝ cushion form.

LIPARI PINWHEEL LAPTOP BAG
(continued from page 44)

4. Add the top and bottom borders to the Mini-Mosaic panel.

Sew the 2½″ × 44½″ strip of Fabric 1 onto the top of the Mini-Mosaic panel. Sew the 4½″ × 44½″ strip of Fabric 1 onto the bottom of the panel. Press the seam allowances away from the center panel. The outer panel of the bag measures 18½″ × 44½″.

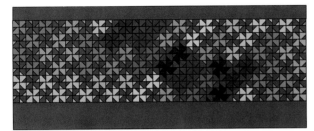

Lipari Pinwheel Laptop Bag outer panel with borders

5. Quilt the outer panel.

Fuse an 18″ × 44″ piece of fusible fleece to the wrong side of the bag front panel, leaving a ¼″ seam allowance all around. Machine quilt as desired. I used gold metallic thread and quilted swirly motifs in the black squares.

6. Quilt the interior lining.

Fuse the 18″ × 44″ remaining piece of fusible fleece to the wrong side of the 18½″ × 44½″ piece of lining Fabric 17, leaving a ¼″ seam allowance exposed around the fusible fleece. Quilt the bag interior lining as desired. I used vertical rows spaced ½″ apart with a variegated thread.

7. Make the inner pocket section.

Fold the 12½″ × 44½″ piece of Fabric 17 in half lengthwise, right side out. Press. Open the fabric piece wrong side up, and align the 6″ × 36″ and 6″ × 8″ pieces of fusible fleece to the fold line, butting the 6″ sides of both pieces end to end, and leaving a ¼″ seam allowance exposed on either end of the fusible fleece. Refold the fabric and fuse the fusible fleece with an iron. Using a machine walking foot, stitch ¼″ from the long fold through all 3 thicknesses at what will be the open top of the inner pockets. Quilt the inner pocket section as desired. I used airy flower motifs made with variegated thread.

8. Mark a line along the 44½″ length on the right side of the bag lining from Step 6, 7½″ from the raw bottom edge. With the fold of the pocket section pointing downward, align the raw edges of the pocket section to this marked line, and pin to hold in place. Stitch the pocket section

onto the lining section, using a ¼″ seam allowance. Turn the pocket section up; then topstitch along the length at the pocket section bottom, ¼″ in from the seam. Staystitch ⅛″ from the raw edge of the sides of the pocket section to hold it in place. Fold (perpendicular to the 44½″ length) to find the halfway line of the bag lining panel; then mark with chalk or a removable marker. Mark a line on the right side of the pocket section 2″ away from the halfway line on both sides. Mark a line across the pocket section 2¼″ in from the outside raw edges. Stitch along these lines through all thicknesses to form the side pockets, starting each of the seams with a backstitch or about ¼″ of small zigzag stitching to reinforce the tops of the pockets. Stitch as many other pockets as you desire along the 2 long parts of the pocket section. Most people find it handy to have a pocket big enough to fit a wallet, another for a cell phone, and so on.

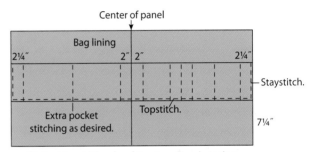

Make Lipari Pinwheel Laptop Bag interior with a lot of pockets.

9. Prepare the handles and removable shoulder strap.

Stitch the 1½″ × 20″ strips of Fabrics 2–16 together lengthwise into a set and then cut in half to measure 10″ × 15½″. Cut 5 segments 1½″ × 15½″ from one set, and stitch these together end to end. From this set, unpick the seam allowances to make 1 piece that is 24 segments long for the shoulder strap and measures 24½″ long and 2 pieces that are 18 segments long for the handles and measure 18½″ long.

Piece strap and handles.

10. Trim to fit and stitch the 1¼″ strips of Fabric 1 onto a long side of each of the 3 strips from Step 9, and the trimmed 2¾″ strips of Fabric 1 to the other long side of each the 3 strips. All 3 strips should now measure 4½″ wide. Stitch a 4½″ × 6″ piece of Fabric 1 to both ends of the long shoulder strap, and a 4½″ × 3″ piece to each end of the handle strips. You now have 2 strips measuring 4½˝ × 23½˝ for the bag handles and 1 strip measuring 4½˝ × 35½˝ for the shoulder strap.

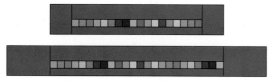

Construct strap and handles.

11. Fold and topstitch the strap and handles.

On the wrong side, position and fuse a 1½˝ heavyweight interfacing strip centered under the long pieced tile section of each of the strap and handle strips. Place the second interfacing strip next to the first, with a small gap between. Fold the long edges of the pieced fabric strips around the edges of the interfacing, and insert a 1½˝-wide strip of fusible fleece under the tile section, inside the fold. Stitch the strips in half lengthwise, topstitching in-the-ditch next to the tiles to create the handles and strap. Trim the interfacing ends to match the fabric.

Use heavyweight fusible interfacing to make bag strap and handles.

Fuse 2 lengths, 4½˝ × 6˝ each, of heavyweight interfacing strips onto the remaining 2 pieces 4½˝ × 6˝ of Fabric 1; then fold and topstitch, similar to the method for the straps and handles, to form the 2 D-ring loops for the removable shoulder strap. All of these should now be 1½˝ wide.

Fold and stitch handles, D-ring sections, and shoulder straps.

12. Make the D-ring holders and shoulder strap.

Fold the 2 pieces 1½˝ × 6˝ from Step 11 in half. Slip a D-ring onto an end of each, with the flat side of the ring positioned in the fold. Topstitch about ½˝ from the fold and backstitch at the beginning and end of the seam. In the same manner, fold over about 3˝ on each end of the long

shoulder strap and then position and stitch the trigger hooks in place. Stitch to secure, using a straight stitch and then again using a zigzag stitch to cover the raw edge.

13. Assemble the bag.

Center and pin the 4 raw ends of the bag handles to the top raw edge of the outer bag panel, with a handle on the front and a handle on the back, keeping the handle ends 6˝ apart. Allow 1˝ of the handles to protrude over the raw edge. (Do not cut off excess!) Staystitch in place by machine, ⅛˝ from the raw edge.

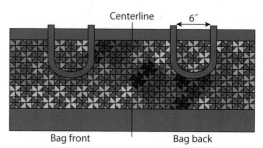

Position bag handles on Lipari Pinwheel Laptop Bag.

14. Fold the bag lining interior and exterior pieces in half, parallel to the 18½˝ side, right sides facing. Pin and stitch the side and bottom seams, leaving 8˝ open at the center bottom of the bag interior lining piece. Align the 2˝ × 2˝ template plastic with the seamlines at the bottom corners of the lining and exterior pieces. Trace around the template with a marking pen. Turn each piece over and repeat the markings.

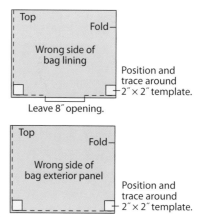

Stitch bag sides and bottoms, and mark around corner templates.

15. With right sides together, squish the corners flat so that the bottom seam and side seam or fold align. Pin, then stitch, along the resulting straight line across each corner. Trim ¼˝ from the seam.

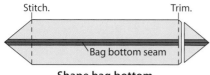

Stitch.   Trim.

Bag bottom seam

Shape bag bottom.

16. Position and pin the 2 shoulder strap D-ring pieces to the inside top of the bag interior lining piece, centering the first piece on the side fold line and the other piece over the side seam. Place the raw ends of the pieces pointing up and the D-ring sections hanging down toward the bag interior. Leave the raw edges of the strips protruding 1″ above the top of the bag. Staystitch D-ring strips in place by machine ⅛″ from the raw edge.

17. Attach the bag feet and bag bottom.

Turn the bag exterior right side out. Cut a small diagonal piece from each corner of the 3½″ × 17″ rectangle of plastic canvas, so there are no sharp, pointy corners to work their way through the fabric of the bag. Mark, then snip out, 4 holes in the plastic canvas for the bag feet. Place the holes 2″ from the short sides and 1″ from the long sides.

Position the plastic canvas inside the bottom of the bag exterior. Mark the position of the 4 holes on the fusible fleece that lines the exterior bag bottom. Use a tailor's awl or large needle to poke a hole through the fabric at the bag bottom at each marked point. Insert a bag foot through each hole in the fabric and the corresponding hole in the plastic canvas; then open and flatten the wings of each bag foot.

18. Stitch the bag together and turn right side out.

Turn the bag exterior right side inward. Turn the bag interior lining

right side outward. Then insert the interior lining into the bag exterior, making sure to have a single side seam on each side of the bag (the lining seam at one end and the bag seam at the other). Pin, then stitch, the bag tops together. Carefully pull the bag through the 8″ opening left in the bottom of the interior lining piece; then insert the bag lining into the bag exterior. Making sure the top seam is well turned out, pin, and then topstitch ¼″ from the seam, catching in the handles and strap loops. Stitch through all thicknesses again 1″ down from the topstitched line, catching the shoulder strap loops with the D-rings so they are hidden inside the bag.

19. Finish the bottom and make the bag stabilizer.

Hand stitch closed the opening that was left at the bottom of the bag lining. Cover the 3½″ × 17½″ foam core with the remnant of batting. Fold and press the 5″ × 36″ piece of Fabric 17 in half so it measures 5″ × 18″ and stitch the 2 long sides together. Insert the covered foam core. Fold in the raw edges and stitch the remaining side closed by hand. Insert this into the bag bottom to add stability and strength to the bag.

20. Make the laptop protective cover bag insert.

Make the fabric base by stitching the 6½″ × 18½″ pieces of fabric together on the long sides of the rectangles to form 2 units of 5 pieces each, a unit for the outside panel of the bag insert and another unit for the lining. Leave an opening of about 8″ at the center of a seam of the lining panel. Each panel measures 18½″ × 30½″.

21. Make the ties for the laptop protective cover bag insert by folding the 1″-wide strip of Fabric 17 in half

lengthwise, wrong sides together, and then bringing in the long raw edges to the center fold and pressing so that it measures ¼″ wide. Topstitch the strip and then cut in half crosswise to form 2 ties.

22. Make the fastening flap by folding the 6½″ × 6½″ piece of Fabric 17 in half, right sides together, and fusing the 3″ × 6″ piece of fusible fleece onto a wrong side along the fold. Stitch the long seams and one short seam, leaving the other short end open. Turn right side out and topstitch ¼″ in from the finished edges. The fastening flap measures 3¼″ × 6″.

23. Assemble the laptop insert. Fuse the 18″ × 30″ piece of fusible fleece to the wrong side of the outside panel, leaving a ¼″ seam allowance all around. Fold each of the panels in half, right sides together, so that each panel measures 15¼″ × 18½″. Fold each of the ties in half crosswise and pin the folded end 1″ down from the top raw edge on the pinned sides of the outside panel. Stitch the sides.

Leave 8″ gap.

Panels for laptop protective cover bag insert

24. With right sides together, pin the fastening flap to the center top edge of the outer laptop bag insert. Align the raw edges of the flap and the top of the outer bag insert. Keep this bag with the wrong side (fusible fleece) out.

Turn the lining right side out and insert it into the outer bag, right sides together. Line up the side seams of both bags. Pin, then stitch, the outer bag to the lining bag through all thicknesses at the top.

25. Turn the lining bag right side out through the 8″ opening left in the lining panel. Pin, then topstitch, ¼″ from the bag top. Stitch hook and loop tape onto the bag front and fastening flap. Tie the removable laptop bag to the inside D-ring holders of the main bag.

Laptop protective cover bag insert

TIP
Use some of the leftover corner triangle tiles to make this 12″ × 12″ block, which can be stitched and stuffed with beans to make a 6″ × 12″ wrist support cushion to go with the laptop bag.

Leftover tiles project

TENLEY'S TEATIME TANGO BOOK COVER
(continued from page 46)

3. Make the book cover.

Stitch the Mini-Mosaic block to the front of the book cover fabric.

Fuse the 5″ × 5″ marked square of fusible web onto the wrong side of the 9½″ × 13¼″ piece of Fabric 10. In the sample, the square was fused 1″ from the top raw edge and 1″ from the left side raw edge of the wrong side of the book cover Fabric 10 rectangle.

Cut a 4″ × 4″ hole along the marked line in the center of the fused fabric. Clip the corners of the cutout to the corners of the 5″ × 5″ marked square. Peel away the paper; then fold and fuse the fabric to the wrong side to create a 5″ × 5″ opening in the front of the book cover fabric. (See Showtime Badge Bag, Steps 4 and 5, pages 70 and 71, for an illustration of a similar technique.)

Use fabric glue to tack the Mini-Mosaic block into position. Use invisible thread to zigzag stitch around the edge of the hole.

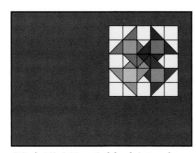

Stitch Mini-Mosaic block into place.

Sandwich the notebook cover with the 9½″ × 13¼″ pieces of batting and muslin, and quilt as desired.

4. Make the book cover pockets.

Fold and press both of the 6½″ × 9½″ pieces of Fabric 10 in half, right sides out, so that the raw edges meet. Each folded piece measures 3¼″ × 9½″. Insert a 3″ × 9″ piece of batting up to the fold line, leaving ¼″ around the raw edges without batting. Quilt as desired.

5. Assemble the book cover.

Position and pin the pockets to the notebook cover sides, right sides together, with the folded pocket edges pointing toward the center. Position and pin the ribbon at the center top of the notebook cover so it runs down the outside cover spine.

Pin the 9½″ × 13¼″ lining piece of Fabric 11 to the book cover and pockets, right sides together. Stitch through all layers, leaving a 6″ opening at the bottom center for turning.

Turn the book cover right side out. Hand stitch the opening closed.

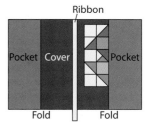

Afterthoughts

TEACHING MINI-MOSAICS

The easiest way to teach Mini-Mosaics is to get class participants to make a Mini-Mosaic block that incorporates most of the basic tile types, such as the Festival block, which is in the Tesserae Sampler Quilt. To save time in class, consider getting participants to precut their fabrics into 1½″ × 1½″ squares and 1½″ × 2½″ rectangles to use in making the tile blanks as described in Making Tile Blanks for Individual Tiles (page 15). The Festival block is also the subject of the free online tutorial on Mini-Mosaics on the Green Mountain Quilt Studio website, www.greenmountainquilts.com.

SOURCES FOR OTHER MINI-MOSAIC PATTERNS

Many traditional block and quilt patterns can be made on a small scale using the Mini-Mosaic method. Here are just a few of the many books you could use to find inspirations to design your own Mini-Mosaic masterpiece:

Jinny Beyer, *The Quilter's Album of Blocks and Borders*

Barbara Brackman, *Encyclopedia of Pieced Quilt Patterns*

Bettina Havig, *Carrie Hall Blocks*

Brenda M. Papadakis, *Dear Jane: The Two Hundred Twenty-Five Patterns from the 1863 Jane A. Stickle Quilt*

OTHER IDEAS FOR MINI-MOSAICS

Beyond the projects in this book, why not make Mini-Mosaic patchwork for your ATCs (Artist Trading Cards), fabric postcards, potholders, beanbags, pincushions, mug rugs, and wrist support cushions to make them extra special? You can also incorporate Mini-Mosaic blocks into bigger quilts with other types of blocks and borders. And a mounted and framed Mini-Mosaic quilt looks great on the wall.

about the author

Despite being born in Massachusetts, Paula Doyle was raised in Brazil, the daughter of Methodist missionary teachers. Her mother taught her how to use a sewing machine at the age of nine, and she made her first patchwork cushion at the age of ten under instruction from her maternal grandmother. After a career in banking and corporate training, Paula moved to London and married Mark Doyle. Their son, Jonathan, was born in 1990 during a seven-year overseas posting to the United States and Canada, which is when quilting became a passion for Paula.

She learned how to make her first sampler quilt in a class at La Maison de Calico, a quilt shop in Pointe-Claire, Quebec. Over the next few years she took more classes, moved to Connecticut, and eventually started to teach patchwork and quilting classes at the local YWCA, at the local quilt guild, and even to a group of nuns in a monastery. On her return to England in 1995 she opened Green Mountain Quilt Shop, where she continued to teach quilting and patchwork classes and to design quilts and quilt patterns. After thirteen years in business, Paula closed the shop to allow her to concentrate solely on designing quilt patterns and teaching. She now works in her garden studio (Green Mountain Quilt Studio) on the banks of the Thames in Surrey, England.

Great Titles *from* C&T PUBLISHING & stashBOOKS.

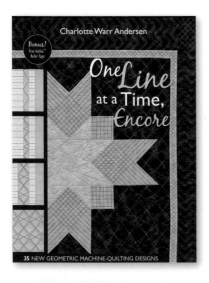

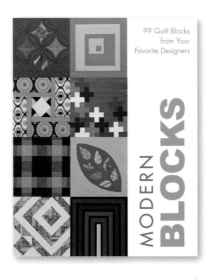

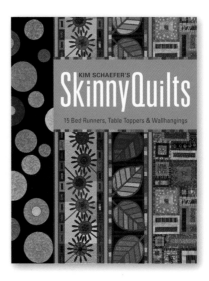

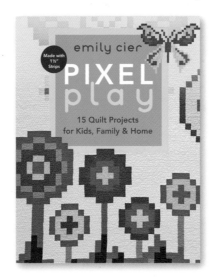

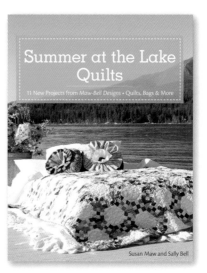

Available at your local retailer or **www.ctpub.com** *or* **800-284-1114**

*For a list of other fine books from C&T Publishing, visit our website
to view our catalog online.*

C&T PUBLISHING, INC.

*P.O. Box 1456
Lafayette, CA 94549
800-284-1114*

*Email: ctinfo@ctpub.com
Website: www.ctpub.com*

*C&T Publishing's professional photography services are now available to
the public. Visit us at www.ctmediaservices.com.*

Tips and Techniques *can be found at www.ctpub.com > Consumer
Resources > Quiltmaking Basics: Tips & Techniques for Quiltmaking & More*

For quilting supplies:

COTTON PATCH

*1025 Brown Ave.
Lafayette, CA 94549
Store: 925-284-1177
Mail order: 925-283-7883*

*Email: CottonPa@aol.com
Website: www.quiltusa.com*

*Note: Fabrics shown may not be currently available, as fabric
manufacturers keep most fabrics in print for only a short time.*